LAS VEGAS BY NIGHT

Frommer's

LAS VEGAS
by Night

BY

JOHN VILLANI

WITH CONTRIBUTIONS FROM
JORDAN SIMON AND
PAUL SHAPIRO

A BALLIETT & FITZGERALD BOOK

MACMILLAN • USA

a disclaimer

Prices fluctuate in the course of time, and travel information changes under the impact of the varied and volatile factors that influence the travel industry. Neither the author nor the publisher can be held responsible for the experiences of readers while traveling. Readers are invited to write to the publisher with ideas, comments, and suggestions for future editions.

about the authors

John Villani is a freelance writer who has been covering the arts, travel, and food in the Southwest since the late 1980s.

Jordan Simon is the author of several guidebooks, as well as co-author of the *Celestial Seasonings Cookbook: Cooking With Tea.*

Paul Shapiro, who contributed to the Casinos and Nightlife chapters, is the co-author of *Paramedic!*, and currently lives in Las Vegas.

Balliett & Fitzgerald, Inc.
Executive editor: Tom Dyja
Managing editor: Duncan Bock
Associate editor: Howard Slatkin
Assistant editor: Maria Fernandez
Editorial assistant: Ruth Ro, Bindu Poulose

Macmillan Travel art director: Michele Laseau

All maps © Simon & Schuster, Inc.

MACMILLAN TRAVEL
A Simon & Schuster Macmillan Company
1633 Broadway
New York, NY 10019

ISBN 0-02-861427-5
Library of Congress information available from Library of Congress.

special sales

Bulk purchases (10+ copies) of Frommer's and selected Macmillan travel guides are available to corporations, organizations, institutions, and charities at special discounts, and can be customized to suit individual needs. For more information write to Special Sales, Macmillan General Reference, 1633 Broadway, New York, NY 10019.

Manufactured in the United States of America

contents

Las Vegas Area Orientation

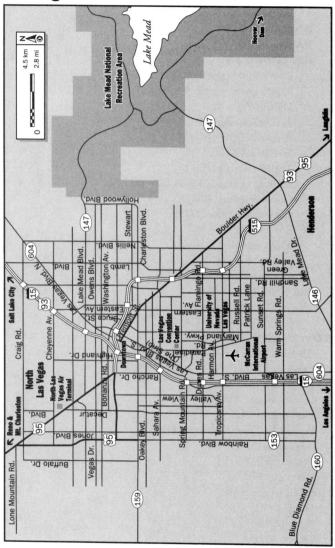

The Strip and Paradise Road Orientation

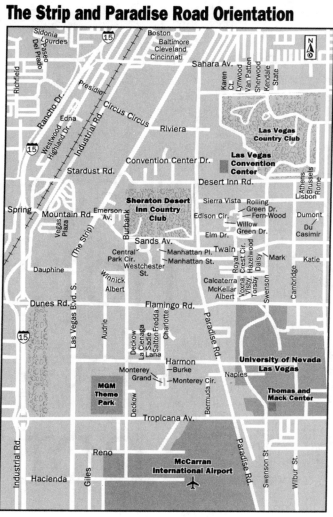

what's
hot,
what's
not

If New York is the city that never sleeps, Las Vegas is the city that never even blinks. This is the place where the casinos pioneered an artificial environment expressly designed to trick the mind into thinking that it's always 11pm and the night is perpetually young. Casinos have no windows or clocks, oxygen is pumped in, and whatever the time you can always hear the soothing sound of coins clattering into metal trays. Vegas is a place so wrapped up in 24-hour culture that even Wal-Mart never closes. It's a city where you can pick up your dry cleaning at 4am or shop for a new pair of fur-covered handcuffs at midnight. In fact, so many restaurants and businesses run round-the-clock that, all the way from the suburbs in swank Green Valley to the cowpoke haven along the Boulder Highway, bars become packed right after the graveyard shift ends at 7am. What Vegas has achieved is unique: action one associates with the night happens here 24 hours a day.

Not only does Vegas never stop to rest, but it never seems to stop growing, either. When the city first started flexing its muscles as a gambling and entertainment mecca, the action centered around **Downtown** in the city's north end along Las Vegas Boulevard. As Vegas grew into full neon bloom, the major casino hotels began to gravitate toward **The Strip**, as the portion of Las Vegas Boulevard south of Sahara Boulevard is known. The Strip divides the creatively named **Westside** (west of The Strip) from the **Eastside** (east of The Strip), while to the north of Downtown lies—you guessed it—**North Las Vegas**. The area south of McCarran Airport used to be known as Henderson, but it has recently renamed itself **Green Valley**, trading in its low-rent image for a new posture as the city's chi-chi bedroom community.

Whether you're talking about condos in Green Valley or casinos on The Strip, these days everything in this incredibly prosperous city seems to be under construction and expanding. Even casino hotels that are already among the world's largest, like the Luxor, Caesars Palace, and the MGM Grand, are undergoing self-financed alterations and improvements costing hundreds of millions of dollars—each. The big casino operations, once headed by gat-toting gangsters and bookmakers, are run today by business-school grads and bookkeepers. Huge corporations have taken over where the mob left off. So if you go expecting a glimpse of the nighttime underworld à la *Casino*, prepare to be disappointed. This is the age of corporate conglomeration, not of shadowy bootlegging, and Vegas isn't about to fall behind the times.

This isn't to say that the influx of big business has drained the life out of this supremely debaucherous city. If anything, it's brought things to a higher pitch. Where there's a wish, a demand, a desire, Vegas will still swiftly adapt to satisfy it. As Vegas has grown into both a bigger urban center and a more diversified resort, nightlife is no longer the province of a few showrooms and bars. New nightclubs have popped up all over town, from the huge and glitzy joints inside the Strip's casinos to blues bars, gay bars, and cowboy bars miles away from any casino's sea of neon. When the urge for surf 'n' turf or a prime rib sandwich strikes at 5am, there are dozens of places that will fill your needs. And the sounds of video poker follow you everywhere, not just in the casinos, fueling much of this growth. More than ever, Vegas supplies nightlife around the clock. The odds are that there's no end in sight.

What's hot

Make that a double (latte)... The tyranny of Seattle has turned a nation of city dwellers into caffeine junkies, and even Las Vegas—the home of free rum-and-cokes and 75-cent Heinekens—has fallen into step with the trend. Espresso carts can be found in most casinos, Starbucks has squeezed itself into a storefront on the Strip, and each shopping center seems to have a coffee bar named Jitters or Java Joe's. Word around town is that liquor consumption is down, so it could be that the new breed of Vegas resident has made a lasting change in this city's once boozy attitude.

Goin' to the go-go, everybody... The seventies revival that has swept the nation is in its full flower in Vegas, a city where the disco lifestyle never really went away. From the boogie music played in the hottest nightclubs to the hip-hugger fashions worn by local clubcrawlers on their nights out, nighttime Las Vegas takes on a bizarre, "Starsky and Hutch" fashion sensibility.

Andre the Giant... Homeboy Andre Agassi, a k a Mr. Brooke Shields, is the one man whom Las Vegas's women most want to join for a night of bliss, according to one local survey. You have a better shot at catching pro tennis's grunge fashion king prowling the streets of Piccadilly during Wimbledon than you do at finding him anywhere in Las Vegas, unless you come here in late September during his one-day fund-raiser, Andre Agassi's Grand Slam for Children, held at either the MGM Grand or the Thomas & Mack Center.

Oh Lord, won'tcha buy me a 36-C... From the moment you deplane at McCarran you'll notice that Las Vegas has a disproportionate number of well-endowed women. Breast augmentation is big business in this town; indeed, Las Vegas has for decades been known as one of the nation's plastic-surgery meccas. More than 50 cosmetic surgery clinics are listed in the local phone book.

Vegas's new image... Now that it's the fastest-growing city in the nation, and prospering tremendously as a result of corporate investments—ITT owns Caesars Palace; Hilton owns Bally's; MGM Grand (a spin-off of the Hollywood giant) owns half of New York, New York— the list goes on and on. Las Vegas has jumped all over a campaign to promote itself as a family resort, a desert version of Disneyland. That's meant a process of pushing out a lot of venerable low-rollers and their smaller-time business ventures (consigning them to nearby Laughlin). And while Las Vegas has a ways to go before it can pronounce itself squeaky clean, there's been nothing less than an overnight turnaround here... one financed by billions of corporate dollars.

I'll take Manhattan... What a concept! Bring a compartmentalized version of the Big Apple to the Mojave Desert, and market it as a way to do Vegas and Gotham all at the same time. Whoomp, there it is: Vegas's newest phenomenon! The 48-story skyscraper-esque towers of New York, New York open their doors in December 1996 with 2,035 hotel rooms, a casino modeled after the floor of the Stock Exchange, a half-scale Statue of Liberty, and a 300-foot-long Brooklyn Bridge. Stand aside for the stampede of tourists and locals alike.

Green Valley Express... Just a few years ago, the tony Vegas suburb known as Green Valley was called Henderson, and had a horrible reputation as a place filled with trailer courts, scorpions, and the shallow graves of mobsters who stepped on the wrong person's toes. Today, with its new name and scrubbed-up image, Green Valley is exploding with growth of all sorts, from $100,000 starter homes to those nutty, only-in-Vegas neighborhood casinos to franchises like Starbucks and The Olive Garden. If you decide to move to Las Vegas, chances are you'll get caught up in Green Valley's superheated real-estate market.

Foot fetishists... For years, several of the nation's largest shoe-industry trade shows have taken place in Las Vegas, and the women of this city have an up-to-date shoe savvy that rivals anything in New York, L.A., or Miami. Leave your Birkenstocks at home, unless you want to be laughed at. This city is a palace of pedicured splendor, a place where even highly paid female attorneys wear 4-inch patent-leather heels.

What's not

Mobsters... Once at the top of Vegas's food chain, organized crime families have hightailed it out of town in the face of this city's corporate takeovers and the resultant demographic shift toward a family-friendly version of the Vegas dream. The combined weight of FBI investigations, too-public exposure of the people behind organized crime's facade, easier profits in the drug trade, and the cash offers from industry titans (it started with Howard Hughes) proved too much for the hoods to bear.

Elvis and Wayne... There are no more Elvis impersonators working the Strip (though you can order one up for a birthday party, no problem). And Wayne Newton has segued nicely into middle age as a real-estate developer and infrequent headline entertainer in places like Caesars Palace and the Las Vegas Hilton. Once again, Vegas's astonishingly fast rate of change has thrown out the old and ushered in the new: the Dennis Millers, Shawn Colvins, and Natalie Coles (well, sorta new) of the world.

Runnin' Rebs... Ever since Tark the Shark had his fins clipped in an NCAA investigation and had to leave town, the UNLV basketball team has struggled to measure up to its glories of years past. Today, when a UCLA or even a BYU blows into town, the Rebs are more often than not KO'd. Oh well, at least courtside seats are easier to come by.

Zoning laws... Anything goes in Las Vegas. Anything, anywhere, anytime you want. The Stratosphere builds a 1,149-foot tower... no problem. MGM Grand builds a 5,005 room mega–casino hotel... no problem. Bellagio announces plans for a 12-acre lake surrounding a 3,500-room casino hotel... no problem. Some local real-estate developer wants to build a hamburger drive-in next to a church... no problem. The only planning that goes on here is figuring out how much money you're going to rake in.

Small is beautiful... In a city where everyone except the occassional sun-addled newcomer gets into their car to go to the corner deli, the best way for a business to attract attention is by being bigger, brighter, and better located than its competition. That's why everything here is three, four, five times the size of similar ventures in other parts of the nation. In Las Vegas, size is everything.

casi

nos 1

Just who do you think pays
the bills around this place?
Sure, Las Vegas is loaded
with restaurants, hotels,
nightclubs, stage shows,
and streetwalkers… but
nightlife, schmightlife—

the bottom line here is gambling. Known as "gaming" among polite society and government regulators, gambling is an all-day, all-night, everywhere-you-go proposition in Las Vegas. From gas-station convenience stores to supermarkets to hair salons to the restaurant atop Mt. Charleston to the concourses of McCarran Airport, there are few places in Las Vegas where you can escape the relentless noise of slot machines and video-poker machines. And why not? As one store owner confided, "Each of these (video-poker) machines makes me $20,000 a month, and if I don't keep them in here, my customers will find another place that has them." And he was just talking about the locals. There's another bottom line here: Whatever the house rules, the house always rules. The odds are not in the gambler's favor (see "Playing the Odds," below).

Gambling is all about the numbers, and has been ever since Nevada legalized it in 1931, making the town a mobster magnet. To the goodfellas in their sharkskin suits and Italian loafers, these slow-talking Westerners in their jeans and cowboy boots must have looked like a comedy routine. But as it turned out, the Nevada politicos knew what they were doing when they grabbed their slice of the gaming industry's pie by creating the State Gaming Commission in 1959. By the time Bobby Kennedy came along as U.S. Attorney General, going *mano-a-mano* with La Cosa Nostra, the writing was on the wall. Within a few years, government authorities from the Department of Justice to the Internal Revenue Service and the F.B.I. came crashing down on Las Vegas, enforcing controls on everything from back-room skimming operations to garbage-pickup services. Smart businessmen that they are, the mobsters started looking for a way to unload their problems and cut their losses. And that's when the corporations stepped in, starting with Howard Hughes in the late 1960s. Thirty years after the eccentric Hughes blew into town, Vegas has not only cleaned up its own act and run nearly all the mobsters and funny-money people out of the casinos (let's call it 97-percent clean), but has also turned its fate over to the starched shirts in the corporate finance departments. It's estimated that Las Vegas casinos will take in approximately $6 billion in profits this year (any wonder why ITT bought Caesars Palace?).

Playing the Odds

You can kiss your rabbit's foot all you want, but the process of winning at a casino's gaming tables involves understanding that being ahead is a temporary situation. Casinos earn their profits on long-term average income. Gambling is a negative-expectation proposition—the casino retains a numerical advantage through what's known as the "odds" (built into the rules of each gambling activity). In other words, you can beat the casino's gambling tables, slots, and video-poker machines in the short run, but if you continue playing, the casino's built-in advantage (a close relative of the law of averages) will catch up with you—relieving you of your winnings and anything else you're foolish enough to fork over. Some casino games—baccarat, blackjack, and craps—have odds that initially place you on nearly even footing with the casino. But to win, they invariably require you to play flawlessly, at full attention; you need experience, knowledge, and discipline. (Some rare situations in video poker and slots also lower the odds to near-even status, but finding and capitalizing on these requires the same sort of experience and expertise as do the table games.) In most casino games, you gamble at odds that overwhelmingly favor the house. These tend to be games that require little (if any) skill or experience; you just plunk down your money and watch to see if you win. You can even have a few drinks under your belt, because you have no control over anything (except for walking out of the casino). The odds are mercilessly stacked against you in keno, roulette, wheel of fortune, some situations in craps, and most video-poker and slot machines. Experience can provide some strategies to better your chances of winning, but a more effective game plan would be learning everything you can about baccarat, blackjack, and craps, and playing them intelligently (and soberly). What's a good set of odds? When the house advantage is anywhere from 0.5 percent (perfect blackjack playing) to 1.4 percent (perfect craps playing). What's a bad set of odds? When the house advantage ranges from 5.26 percent (perfect roulette playing) to 20 percent (perfect keno playing). Important! These odds are for perfect play. If you make mistakes during play, all the odds shoot up to astronomical levels and the die is truly cast—as in a pall over your vacation.

How To Learn

Fortunately for the uninitiated, there are free lessons offered at many casinos, aimed at introducing people to the games. These lessons are held late mornings or early afternoons, the slack periods before most of the casinos' serious action begins. Depending on the casino, you'll find everything from craps to blackjack and roulette instruction taking place in these one-hour sessions, plus an hour or so of "slow play" when the tables maintain low dollar limits and run at a pace allowing newcomers to take their time making decisions and to ask questions of the dealers and pit staff. To find out about which gambling lessons are offered at what times by a hotel, check with the front desk or look for the sections in freebie publications such as *Today in Las Vegas* or *Casino Player* detailing which lessons are offered around town.

Dos and Don'ts

Rule number one: *Never* gamble with money you can't afford to lose. And we advise not playing for money when you don't really understand the game—it's tough to learn when you're playing with real money. You also need a sound strategy *and* a money-management plan if you have hopes of not losing everything. You'll end up "luckiest" by being a disciplined low roller. Say your bankroll is between $50 and $200; if you start with $50 and find yourself up $25, take the total and take a break (even if it's only walking around to the high-rollers' area to watch the rich and reckless). Do this often enough and keep within your limit, and at the end of a three-day visit, you'll be likelier to have pocketed a few hundred bucks in profit. If you lose that first $50 immediately, *do not* dig deeper into your wallet in the hope you'll win it back. Walk away. Relax (desperation improves neither your mood nor your luck). Try one more session later, playing conservatively, using your head and the experience you've gained. Think of gambling merely as a recreational pursuit, don't stake next month's rent on making a big killing (you'll get killed), and enjoy the people-watching in the town's hilariously overdone casinos. One last note: Not all casinos and casino games are alike. In other words, different casinos may have different rules and payoffs for the same game. By starting out playing correctly, you may actually lower your expected losses considerably. For those who think they can gain an edge by reading up on the topic (and you can to a point), call the Gambler's Book Club (tel 702/382–7555; 630 S. 11th St.), a local institution which seems to have everything ever written on the subject.

The Lowdown

Casinos crass... If it weren't for its freakishly over-the-top design schemes, Vegas would be a lot like Reno or even Atlantic City (shudder). Vegas is a desert flower invented by cocktail-impaired Hollywood designers. Learn to love it. A slot is a slot is a slot, but you'll definitely blink twice at Rio Rita, Carmen's glowing cousin (replete with fruit-salad hat), who overlooks the **Rio** casino, west of the Strip, from a thatched hut bursting with garish stuffed toucans and parrots. Add the squinty bright lighting, and you'd swear you were at a 1940s Hollywood premiere of a gaudy Technicolor B movie. Speaking of parrots, the stuffed versions over at **Treasure Island** actually wear eye patches. Shiver me timbers (or just shiver at the crassness). But why stop there? Let's add treasure chests spilling with pirate booty in every corner, woven-rattan ceilings, loot (mostly fake pieces-of-eight) actually littering the carpets like sawdust in a bar, ships' figureheads, and lots of marine-themed artwork. The **California** isn't so much lacking in taste as it is schizophrenic. Since it caters to masses of visitors flying in on charters from Hawaii, dealers wear aloha shirts and Don Ho songs have been known to float through the otherwise elegant marble-floored, crystal-chandeliered space. If you want to commune with the spirit of Bugsy Siegel, head off the Strip to the **Flamingo Hilton**. But be warned: it could give you a headache (if a losing streak doesn't), with its glaring orange and pink neon lights and fake skylights with painted-on skies. Out on Fremont Street, the **Showboat** has re-created itself by duplicating Bourbon Street during Mardi Gras (minus the drunken revelers and transvestite floats): flowered trellises and vast floral murals adorn the bingo parlor. On the Strip, **Harrah's** chimes in with its own riverboat motif, including French Quarter facades and dealers garbed as turn-of-the-century gamblers. Within its Egyptian-inspired pyramid, the **Luxor** not only favors red, red, and more red as its dominant color, but also etches hieroglyphics on the walls and strews replicas of artifacts from the Temple of Karnak throughout. Even the slot-machine areas feature sphinxes and King Tut heads. **Excalibur** will make you feel like a Connecticut Yankee in King Arthur's Court: stained-glass panels, suits of armor, heraldic banners (in satin and velvet no less), dragons, and enormous iron and gilded chandeliers. **Fitzgeralds** is too cute for words: Gamblers are greeted by a leprechaun, green predominates (including shamrocks stenciled everywhere), and you can even rub a piece of the real Blarney stone (but it won't help you sweet-talk a dealer into letting you move your chips once play has started). Wanna visit a rain forest with thatched huts? Of all the high-end behemoths, you should not miss the **Mirage**, which went bananas with its Polynesian decor. Meanwhile, the **Las Vegas Hilton** still has that Elvis-slept-here look. And who knows, maybe Captain Kirk will beam his own interior decorator aboard when the Hilton's $70-million Star Trek wing opens. Let's not forget the latest Vegas craze: building a city-themed casino. Yes, that's right, we're talking about **New York, New York**, the Strip's latest mega–casino hotel, home to the largest version of the Statue of Liberty west of Newark. Is it Greenwich Village you like? How about the razzle-dazzle of the stock exchange, or even the Brooklyn Bridge? Of course, you know they'll never have the budget problems suffered by the real thing. And if you ever wondered what a turn-of-the-century bordello looked like, stop by the **Barbary Coast**. You won't find out, but you will see miles of red velour and globe chandeliers. And even though the **Tropicana** is noted for its gorgeous stained-glass archway and art nouveau fixtures, these seem somewhat incongruous amid the lush jungle greenery; it's a slightly seedy, totally wacked-out Vegas-in-Samoa jungle theme.

Casino beautiful... The **Golden Nugget**'s complete overhaul has transformed it into worthy competition for the real Grand Casino in Monte Carlo, with Tivoli lighting and stained-glass panels. The **Hacienda** almost overdoes the Mexican theme, but the gleaming white adobe walls, brightly colored still-life paintings, and serapes are an unusual, refreshing change. The **Hard Rock** gets points for trying to be the coolest, hippest hangout, with

Harley Davidson motorcycles sitting above banks of slots, Sting's leather jacket mounted inside a plexiglass showcase (among other celebrity mementos), and a very stylish (and somehow intimate) round bar sitting smack in the middle of the gaming area. Makes you forget you're even in a casino. **Caesars Palace** gets credit only for its surprisingly restrained use of color (black, gold, and ivory). The **MGM Grand**'s claim to fame is its Hollywood design themes that work most (but not quite all) of the time. These include the 63-color rainbow, seven-story Emerald City, yellow brick road, and robotic Oz characters. The **Monte Carlo** is rather stark, even though it struggles to appear luxurious. Surprisingly, somebody here payed attention to the "less is more" school of design—a blessed relief from so much opulence masquerading as taste elsewhere. Love those white-and-brass pay phones. The **Barbary Coast** is sophisticated, imaginative, even witty, with over $2 million worth of exquisite stained-glass skylights. The **Imperial Palace** isn't quite the Chinese wing at the Met, but the New Year's dragon-themed ceilings and wind-chime chandeliers are almost soothing.

The friendliest li'l casino(s) in Nevada... One gambler's friendly pit boss may be another's scourge. That said, the smaller, more local establishments tend to be friendlier and less stuck-up than the big Strip mega-resorts. Which isn't to say that if you're a big bettor, the pit staff at **Caesars** and the **Mirage** won't bend over backwards and try to be friendly. But for the small-stakes player who wants to spend a few hours gambling, have a good time, not lose too much, and not deal with the pressure some other casinos apply, a few places stand out. If you can handle the cigarette smoke at **Arizona Charlie's**, this locals' casino on Decatur Boulevard caters nicely to the low rollers, with friendly dealers, decent table games, and slot machines. Slightly out of town, off U.S. 15 and Blue Diamond Road, **Boomtown** sports a cowboy motif. The tables are relaxed, with low minimums, low pressure, and easy comps. At the youthful (read: loud) **Hard Rock**, you won't find too many blue-haired ladies fighting over the slot machines—or the older, craggy table players found at most downtown casinos. Just off the Strip and a whole lot more low-key than most Strip places, **Maxim** has been a favorite for years, though their blackjack game recently underwent a horrific change in rules, increasing

CASINOS ⟩ THE LOWDOWN

the gambler's disadvantage. It has liberal food comps, and the dealers are usually willing to give free advice to low-stakes players. Friendly pit bosses and hotel managers are a refreshing deviation from the Vegas norm. With its Wild West–themed decor, **Sam's Town** on Boulder Highway caters to a nice mixture of tourists and locals. It's low on pressure and has live country music every night. Of the big-time casinos, the quietly tony **Las Vegas Hilton** always makes you feel like a high roller, even when you walk in there with a bum's bankroll.

And now for something completely different... If you're happiest hanging out in a bus depot and always wished there were slot machines in the bowels of Penn Station, then **Slots-a-Fun** is your type of place. Always packed, this is truly the bus station of casinos, with foot-long dogs and 75-cent Heinekens for sale. Come here for super-low-stakes tables. If you're wearing a shirt with buttons, you're overdressed—part of the fun is smearing mustard and pickle relish on your clothes. When you're done with your serious gambling, dinners, and shows, Slots-a-Fun is where you really let yourself go.

Where the high rollers roam... First: not downtown. Second: not on the Boulder Strip. That's right, high rollers like finding their fun on *the* Strip. Some places are especially geared toward servicing high rollers with every little perk imaginable. They'll set aside special rooms at the edges of their casino's gambling areas, or they'll have them upstairs in a special invitation-only suite. It's fun to stand outside the accessible high-roller areas—usually separated from the rest of the casino by a low, marble railing—to watch the action inside. It's great people-watching and an education in playing styles, and who knows when you'll ever be that close to a $1,000 chip again? The high-rollers' casinos are **Caesars Palace**, the **Las Vegas Hilton**, the **Mirage**, **MGM Grand**, and, to a lesser degree, **Bally's**, **Rio**, and the **Hard Rock**. The recently opened and under-construction casinos such as **Monte Carlo**, **New York, New York**, and **Bellagio** are, contrary to their appearances, not targeted toward high rollers, even though their concepts seem to be oriented that way. Instead, these places are all aimed at the middle-market (albeit the upper end of the middle-market), because that is increasingly the source of this city's tourism growth. Needless to say, the high-roller casinos do their utmost to present an elegant face to their clients. The Mirage's rain forest makes you think you've stumbled into an island paradise, while Caesars's statuary and toga-clad staff give you delusions of imperial grandeur. The over-the-top decor is appropriately debauched in a Caligula sort of way.

Bottom feeding... The Vegas term for a low-rollers' haven is a "grind joint." In general, the downtown casinos (with the notable exception of the Golden Nugget) fall into this category. The casinos on Boulder Highway, which cater mostly to Vegas's resident population of seniors and locals, are packed with low rollers, especially on weekends. But if you enter one of these establishments, be forewarned that Vegas locals tend to know how to maximize their chances of winning at the gaming tables. So watch and learn a few pointers, if you've got the time. In Glitter Gulch, at the **Gold Spike** you can try fighting for one of the two dozen or so seats in front of the last penny slots in town. On the Strip, let's start with **Slots-a-Fun**, a place so oriented toward low rollers, it's a comedy unto itself. If you miss going in here during your stay in Vegas, you'll be missing out on one of the best free shows in town—the people-watching. Flanking Slots-a-Fun are **Circus Circus** (its owner) and the **Stardust**, both very attractive to the low-roller crowd. Across the street, the Strip's first high-rise hotel, the **Riviera**, gets its share of low rollers, as does the **Barbary Coast**, a low-end casino known to throw out blackjack players who even appear to be counting cards. Off the Strip on Flamingo Road, **Maxim** is a nice, small casino hotel with clean rooms and an air of class. They're liberal with complimentary goodies (See "Comps—the ugly truth," below) and make an effort to know the names of frequent gamblers. Right next door is **Bourbon Street**, only worth visiting for its low minimums.

How to name your game... You need to decide which game suits you best. Remember, you're here to have fun (we sincerely hope). Many experienced gamblers prefer the craps tables because the action's much more sociable, and an alert, knowledgeable strategist can bring his odds of winning up to near even with the casino's. Blackjack tables aren't as gregarious a place as the craps tables, and

CASINOS ⟨ THE LOWDOWN

some are loaded with cranky guys chain-smoking ciga-rettes—or worse, cheap cigars. If you look around, you can usually find a smoke-free section in most casinos, as well as blackjack tables that aren't infected by scowling, constipated-looking gamblers. The dealer will often be talkative and helpful with your questions regarding card-playing or betting strategies. If you end up sitting at a blackjack table where the dealer's trying hard to make sure you're having a good time, be sure to tip him or her well when you leave. Roulette can be fun, as long as you play it as a short-term amusement, and use a smart bet-ting strategy to prevent the odds from going too far against you. The action around the roulette wheel can be friendly and lively. Since you're playing against the other people at the poker table, there's usually very little social-izing (no surprise, with everyone after each other's bank-rolls). Sometimes, the atmosphere gets so thick, you half expect a disgruntled player to draw a gun à la "Maverick." Slot- and video-poker machines are conducive to noth-ing except staring at a screen or a bank of spinning reels. Someone should probably research the long-term effects of the action on your gray matter; if you check out the plethora of grimly determined retirees who park their butts at slot machines, chain-smoking and sucking up the casino's free drinks, you just may be able to stay away from slots and video poker for the rest of your living days.

Crapping out... Basically, craps is fairly consistent from casino to casino. The rules are the same, as are most of the payoffs. The only real fluctuation is in the odds that the casino offers when you "back up" your "come out" bet. (If you don't know what that means, you probably should not be playing this game.) For the most part, "back-up odds" range from double to 10-times odds. (On Wednes-day nights **Binion's Horseshoe** offers 100-times odds; normally their odds are 20 times.) You don't get any addi-tional advantage with increased odds—only the ability to win or lose that much faster. Casinos that offer 10-times odds include **Sam's Town, Boulder Station,** and **Circus Circus.** The downtown casinos offer slightly better pay-offs on the hard numbers: 31:1 for snake eyes and boxcars (2 and 12), and 16:1 for 11s. Strip casinos traditionally offer 30:1 and 15:1, respectively. Just about every casino on the Strip and downtown offers craps lessons, but you should always call ahead to confirm times and the location of the table where the lessons take place (these casinos are too big for guessing). Some of the friendliest craps tables are operated by **Bally's**, the **Aladdin**, and **Sam's Town** (where you'll receive a "Certified Gambler" certificate after the lessons are completed).

Hit me... Blackjack is still the most popular table game in Las Vegas, but it's amazing how much variance there is from table to table, casino to casino, when it comes to this classic. Some casinos allow multiple splitting of pairs, some don't. Some casinos allow doubling down after splits, some don't. Some offer surrender. At some tables the dealer sticks on *all* 17s; some consider a soft 17 (ace/six) a seven and continue hitting. Each rule variation affects the player's bottom line. Some of these rules are favorable to the casino, some the player; carefully choosing which table to play at can considerably reduce your disadvantage. Try to play at a casino that allows re-splits, doubles after splitting, and surrender, and where the dealer must stick on all 17s. For the most part, the Strip casinos offer better rules than the downtown establishments. They also have the more expensive (higher minimum bets) games. The **Las Vegas Hilton** offers rules that yield some of the best odds in town for players. The **Mirage**, **Treasure Island**, **MGM Grand**, the **Desert Inn**, **Caesars Palace**, and, more recently, the **Tropicana** all deal a favorable game. For lower-stakes players, the **Boomtown**, **Excalibur**, **Four Queens**, **Sam's Town**, and the **Stardust** all offer decent games. Downtown seems, for some reason, to be a great place to learn a thing or two about flipping cards; head over to **Fitzgeralds**, **Four Queens**, or **Lady Luck** to get a sense of how the game's played.

One-armed banditry... What's there to say? Slots are the ultimate in electronic morphine. Eventually, no matter how much you may initially win (assuming you initially win anything), you are going to lose it again. Which casino has the "loosest" slots? Almost everyone advertises "Loosest Slots on the Strip." Contrary to popular belief, legend, and cosmic inspiration, we've been unable to come up with definitive differences. A number of locals tout their slot payoffs at **Arizona Charlie's**, **Sam's Town**, and the **Showboat**. The **Flamingo Hilton** offers slot machines with Caddies and Lincoln Continentals as jackpots, lending new meaning to "Wheel of Fortune." The slightest whiff of "loose slots" action sets off a Vegas version of the

Senior Olympics, clogging the slot rows with over-60s . If you're wondering whether to seek out or to avoid a machine that has just paid off, the jury's out on this one. But mathematics would imply that your odds of winning are the same no matter when you pull the lever. If you want to maximize your winnings when you do in fact win, try to find a machine that is plugged into the megabucks system. This progressive payoff connects a series of machines across many casinos, to give off huge jackpots. On one weekend in September 1996, $6.3 million dollars was paid out in two Nevada casinos. Only two casinos bother teaching you the intricacies of lowering the odds at slot machines (more than half the city's gambling revenue comes in through the slots—why tinker with a good thing?). So before throwing all your dough down the throat of a one-armed bandit, slot an hour for lessons at **Four Queens**, downtown, or **Harrah's**, on the Strip.

Spinning wheels... The best bet for roulette is the **Monte Carlo Hotel and Casino**. It's a simple game, really. A little white ball spins around a wheel and then finally falls into 1 of 38 holes. The usual roulette table has 36 colored numbers—half red, half black—and the green-colored 0 and 00 (for a total of 38 numbers). The payoff for hitting a single number is 35:1, but the odds are really 37:1. If betting on red or black is your preference, remember that there are 18 red, 18 black, and two green numbers. This means that, even though a successful color bet pays 1:1, there are 18 winning colors and 20 losing colors—basically a 5-percent disadvantage, which is huge. But there are a few roulette tables in Las Vegas that have *only one zero* (they're called "single-zero" roulette tables). They've got the same payoffs, but now instead of a 5-percent house advantage, you're only facing a 2- to 3-percent disadvantage; by choosing the right roulette table, you cut your disadvantage in half. The Monte Carlo is the only casino where *every* wheel has a single zero. A few other casinos offer some single-zero roulette wheels (but are expensive), including **Caesars Palace**, the **Mirage**, the **Las Vegas Hilton**, and **MGM Grand**, where the wheel sits in the high-roller pit with $500 minimums.

Poker (real and fake)... For serious poker players, **Binion's Horseshoe**, downtown, is the first choice; it's home of the annual world poker championship. Low ceilings and a chandelier hang over a dark, smoke-filled floor, where emphysemic-looking 40- to 50-year-olds gather to take each other's money. A cautionary note about poker: The house takes the ante on every hand, so the casino makes the same money no matter who wins. It's every gambler for himself, and at a table of strangers, you have no idea how much better your opponent is than you—or even if he or she might be in cahoots with other players at the table. These variables mean that you have little control of the odds. But if you're on the Strip and want to try your hand, the rowdy **Riviera** is the best place to play or learn; off the Strip, **Sam's Town** has a lot of low-to-medium stakes poker tables. Meanwhile, video poker has become one of the most popular types of slot machines. "V.P.," as the in crowd refers to it, has invaded every casino in Las Vegas. Of course, you might as well play real slots. Without the human element—that is, getting cleaned out by a dour-looking bruiser who has a computer for a brain—poker is not poker. Still, even we have to confess to stopping at a machine for a hand or two and snapping out of the video-induced fever hours later, having drained $20 in quarters. In theory, the odds of getting a royal flush (the best possible outcome) should be the same from machine to machine. However, it is possible to find dramatic differences in machine payoffs. Search out a machine that is hooked into a "progressive" type of system. Also try to find a machine that pays 6:1 for a flush and 9:1 for a full house; most pay out 5:1 and 8:1, respectively. Some machines have deuces wild, some only a joker wild; some have special payoff bonuses for four of a kind in aces or eights. **Arizona Charlie's**, **The Santa Fe Hotel** (North Las Vegas), the **Hacienda**, the **Stardust**, **Four Queens**, and **Fitzgeralds** all seem to have a large number of 6/9 video-poker games, and the **Fiesta Hotel and Casino** claims to be the royal-flush capital, advertising more winners than any other casino. Be an alert consumer. Sometimes it's possible to find a machine with better payoffs right next to another not-as-good machine. It's worth taking the time to search for the best machines. It's your money (at least for now).

Smokiest casinos... The hands-down winners of Vegas's indoor smog award are the downtown casinos, especially places like **Binion's Horseshoe**, **Fitzgeralds**, and **Four Queens**. These grind joints have seen their best days come and go, but still fill an important niche in this city's gambling scene: small, friendly spots that make everyone from seniors to five-kid families feel welcome. But small also translates into stifling: There's more smoke here than at the big *EFX* show when Michael Crawford comes on as Merlin. Down on the Strip you'll definitely want to bring your oxygen tank into **Slots-a-Fun**. Be sure to wheel it next door to the **Stardust** or across the street to the **Riviera**, too.

Freshest air... Downtown, the **Golden Nugget** has poured tens of millions of dollars into its remake, and thankfully it didn't skimp on the ventilation system. The **California** is also a breath of fresh air, but more for its funky, open "Hawaiian Islands" decor and equally open, friendly attitude. On the Strip, the **Las Vegas Hilton**, **Flamingo Hilton**, **Monte Carlo**, **MGM Grand**, **Luxor** and the towering **Stratosphere** have all installed millions of dollars' worth of smoke-sucking equipment. In some of the newer casinos, the air is so fresh it's rumored that a mixture of oxygen and refrigerated air is pumped onto the gambling floor every 20 minutes or so, starting at 9pm and continuing till 3am. Ironically, the atmosphere feels hospital-antiseptic as a result.

Comps—the ugly truth... One of the great joys of gambling in Las Vegas casinos is getting comps. Complimentaries—"comps," in the casino vernacular—are what the casino gives you for nothing. All you have to do for this reward is gamble at their tables for a while. So be careful: You may end up losing several hundred dollars in order to qualify for a free $5 buffet dinner. What kind of comp you receive depends on where you gamble, for what stakes, and for how long. Large and expensive casinos that see themselves as classy, such as **MGM Grand** and **Caesars Palace**, for example, require that you gamble at least $25 a hand at the blackjack tables, for four hours, before they even consider comping you dinner. Smaller, mid-sized casinos such as **Harrah's**, **Maxims**, and **Boomtown** require less time and lower minimums. If you're only betting $2 a hand for half an hour, don't expect any casino to cough up a gourmet dinner with wine. But if you place bets that are moderate ($25 a hand) or large ($100 a hand), make sure the casino people know who you are. To do this, get rated, which is quite easy at any casino. When you initially purchase chips (buy in) at the table, the dealer will call the amount to the pit boss. Simply tell the

dealer or supervisor that you wish to have you[r]
They'll take your name and birth date, or address, o[r]
you fill out a small form… and voila! you're being rated b[y]
the casino. Then, every time you sit down at a gaming
table, give them your rating card (issued by the casino).
You'll slowly accrue points towards dinners, or rooms, or
what have you. If the casino personnel come over to you
and ask if they "can do anything for you," that's casino-
speak for offering you a comp. If they don't come to you,
go over to them. If they tell you that your play didn't qualify, ask them what type of play would. If they're too vague
or their requirements seem unreasonable, find another
casino. There are lots of them. And somewhere in this
town there is a casino that will reward your level of action.

If you think the casino's cheating… Just think about
it: the payoff for a cheating casino is probably only a few
thousand bucks, while if they're caught, their punishment
will be millions of dollars in lost revenue from being
closed or fined by the regulatory agencies. The resulting
bad publicity alone could severely cripple a casino. What
it comes down to is that the casinos already have a very
real and substantial advantage over you. They don't need
to cheat. If you honestly believe that something is not
quite right, or if you just have a gnawing, sneaky, completely unsubstantiated suspicion… leave. There are lots
of other craps, blackjack, and roulette tables in Las Vegas.

If you're thinking about cheating… In a word, *don't*.
We know, it seems only fair: You've lost so much money.
And they have so much money. (A large chunk of it is
yours.) But the casinos like to keep it that way. If you think
it's easy to slip one of your own dice into the craps game,
or replace a few cards at the blackjack table with your own,
or place a few extra chips on the table when you have a
winning hand, you're wrong. Besides the dealers, who are
trained to look out for cheating, the floor supervisors are
watching for it, too, as are the pit bosses and security offi-
cers. Not to mention the ever-present "eye in the sky,"
which not only looks for cheaters, but also records them
on videotape—which will result in your arrest. The casinos, the police, the courts, and the prisons out here take
cheating seriously. The judges in Nevada are elected with
support (read: money) from the casinos, so they may be
particularly unsympathetic to your pleas for mercy.

The Index

Aladdin Casino Hotel. If you want to experience a taste of what Las Vegas was like in its 1960s heyday, stay a few nights at this glitzy, slightly frayed-at-the-edges casino hotel. Elvis and Priscilla were married in the owner's penthouse way back when, and to this day honeymooners and some high rollers requiring privacy fill the secluded suites behind this 1,100-room complex. One of the Aladdin's strong points is its 7,000-seat Theatre for the Performing Arts, which hosts concerts, touring Broadway shows, and headliner entertainment.... *Tel 702/736–0111. 3667 Las Vegas Blvd. S.*

Arizona Charlie's. One of the local folks' favorite casinos, Arizona Charlie's has Southwestern-themed decor, a liberal comps policy, and lots of low-roller goodies such as nickel slots and free drinks galore.... *Tel 702/258–5200. 740 S. Decatur Blvd.*

Bally's Las Vegas. This 3,000 room casino hotel on the Strip was once the MGM Grand (it's still connected to the new MGM Grand by a mile-long monorail, Vegas's stab at mass transit). Bally's is a well-run operation that fills an important niche: It's not as chic (or pretentious) as Caesars or the MGM Grand, yet is more upscale than places like the Rio and Flamingo Hilton—somewhere between white collar and black tie. Be sure to catch the multicolored fountains in front as you glide into the casino's entrance from the Strip along the 1,000-foot moving sidewalk.... *Tel 702/739–4111. 3645 Las Vegas Blvd. S.*

Barbary Coast Casino Hotel. This grind joint pulls most of its business in off the Strip from tourists wandering between Bally's, the Aladdin, and the Flamingo Hilton. It has a

McDonalds, which gives you an idea of the size of the typical bet.... *Tel 702/737–7111. 3595 Las Vegas Blvd. S.*

Bellagio Casino Hotel. When this mega-casino hotel, built on the site of what used to be the Dunes Hotel, opens its doors in 1998, it will bring 3,000 more hotel rooms to the Strip, as well as a 12-acre lake filled with the water that would have been used on the Dunes's fairways and greens.... *Tel 702/791–7111. 3400 Las Vegas Blvd. S.*

Binion's Horseshoe Casino Hotel. This downtown Vegas classic is a must-see for its gambling tables loaded with real-life cowboys and cowgirls, as well as a great 99-cent shrimp cocktail and an all-night, $3 steak dinner.... *Tel 702/ 382–1600. 128 E. Fremont St.*

Boomtown Casino Hotel. The cowboy past of Nevada is celebrated at Boomtown, a down-home, family-friendly sort of place favored by the RV crowd. Always jammed during rodeo week.... *Tel 702/263–7777. 3333 Blue Diamond Rd.*

Boulder Station Casino Hotel. The huge sportsbook is filled with serious local gamblers nearly every day. There are also 12 state-of-the-art movie screens in its multiplex cinema.... *Tel 702/432–7777. 4111 Boulder Hwy.*

Bourbon Street Casino Hotel. One of the Strip's smallest operations keeps its head above water by doling out great deals through coupon books, slot clubs, reportedly loose slots, etc.... *Tel 702/737–7200. 120 E. Flamingo Rd.*

Caesars Palace. Where every man and woman can feel like an emperor. Caesars's design theme may be overdone—marble mania!—but when it comes to Vegas-style quality and class, this is the place that has set the standards for over 30 years, and everyone in town knows it. High rollers, beautiful people, gourmet restaurants, rocking, rollicking clubs, and, yes, the Telly Savalas Players Club—all here under the vast roof of Vegas's numero uno.... *Tel 702/731–7110. 3750 Las Vegas Blvd. S.*

California Casino Hotel. The reason Hawaiian Airlines flies into Vegas several times daily is, in large part, to ferry Aloha State gamblers in and out of the California. Very friendly, and

CASINOS ⟋ THE INDEX

serves the island's favorite foods.... *Tel 702/385–1222. 12 Ogden Ave.*

Circus Circus Casino Hotel. It's a zoo, it's an amusement park, its a grind joint, it's a high-wire, three-ring circus—it's way, way over the top. That totally confusing atmosphere (jugglers, clowns, and acrobats circling the casino—perhaps a fiendishly clever trick to distract you and ruin your concentration) is what makes the Circus Circus experience so memorable; don't come here expecting a moment's rest.... *Tel 702/734–0410. 2880 Las Vegas Blvd. S.*

Desert Inn Casino Hotel. Known for having one of the Strip's more sophisticated, quieter environments, the Sheraton (they own the joint) Desert Inn is perhaps best known as the place where reclusive billionaire Howard Hughes settled in for a long stay. He liked it so much that he bought the place.... *Tel 702/733-4444. 3145 Las Vegas Blvd. S.*

Excalibur Casino Hotel. This place takes the Middle Ages to heart, dressing its staff like they're extras in a Robin Hood film. A huge casino hotel with a red-and-black interior color scheme, Excalibur's crowd is nearly all tourists sucked in by its jaw-dropping facade.... *Tel 702/597–7777. 3850 Las Vegas Blvd. S.*

Fiesta Casino Hotel. This very popular North Las Vegas operation is famous for having a drive-through sportsbook as well as Garduno's Cantina, a New Mexico–style restaurant serving the best Mexican food in the city.... *Tel 702/631–7000. 2400 N. Rancho Dr.*

Fitzgeralds Casino Hotel. *The* place to hang out on St. Paddy's Day in Vegas is an Irish-themed casino hotel where you can rub a genuine chunk of the Blarney Stone for good luck before hitting the tables. Known for its "loose slots" and huge parking garage (important in crowded downtown Vegas), Fitzgeralds is a favorite with locals who know a good deal.... *Tel 702/388–2400. 301 E. Fremont St.*

Flamingo Hilton Casino Hotel. Neon—pink, turquoise, and yellow—is all it takes to draw people off the Strip and into this historic (by Vegas standards) place, famous for being Bugsy Siegel's triumph (and downfall). Filled with middle-Americans.... *Tel 702/733–3111. 3555 Las Vegas Blvd. S.*

Four Queens Casino Hotel. This downtown casino advertises itself as the home of Big Bertha, the world's largest slot machine. The best thing Four Queens has going for it is the Monday Night Jazz jam session (see Nightlife), which pulls together some of the city's best musicians as well as an appreciative, enthusiastic audience of friendly music lovers.... *Tel 702/385–4011. 202 E. Fremont St.*

Gambler's Book Club. Though its storefront location closes at 5pm, you can call this place's 800-number to get a catalogue of all the latest Vegas guidebooks, gambling tip sheets, and even gambling software.... *Tel 800/634–6243. 630 S. 11th St. Open 10am to 5pm, closed Sun.*

Gold Spike Casino Hotel. A grind-joint reputation keeps this low-rollers' paradise in the green. Like an airport lounge during Christmas week, this place is always crowded, and the folks here are always looking to cash in on some deal; if you routinely give up your plane seats for a later flight and a free round-trip ticket, this may be the place for you.... *Tel 702/384–8444. 400 Ogden Ave.*

Golden Nugget Casino Hotel. The class act of downtown, this elegant casino hotel has completely renovated its casino and 1,907 rooms. The Nugget can hold its own against anything on the Strip in every category.... *Tel 702/386–8121. 129 E. Fremont St.*

Hacienda Casino Hotel. In any other city, the 840-room Hacienda would qualify as a mega-resort, but from its location at the lower end of the Strip all the Hacienda can do is stare northward at its 2,000 and 3,000-room big sisters. Probably best known as current Vegas showroom magician Lance Burton's training ground.... *Tel 702/739-8911. 3950 Las Vegas Blvd. S.*

Hard Rock Casino Hotel. Vegas's swankest, hippest atmosphere, courtesy of the Hard Rock's upbeat take on the memorabilia-driven decor that made its international chain of restaurants famous. Young crowd, great music, stiff drinks, and a place to see-and-be-scene.... *Tel 702/693–5000. 4455 Paradise Rd.*

Harrah's Casino Hotel. There may be no more hospitable place on the Strip than Harrah's. And now that its tired decor is being redone with the help of $450 million from casino cash flow, Harrah's will soon be able to compete with the glitziest. A top bet for a quick gambling lesson, as the dealers are congenial and the parking user-friendly and literally easy-come, easy-go.... *Tel 702/369–5000. 3475 Las Vegas Blvd. S.*

Imperial Palace. One of the Strip's silliest themes has to be the Imperial Palace's attempt at casting itself in a Ming Dynasty emperor's robes. On the other hand, it's a gimmick that works wonder for the joint's restaurants... and there's a great car collection on one enclosed level of the parking garage.... *Tel 702/731–3311. 3535 Las Vegas Blvd. S.*

Lady Luck Casino Hotel. Beloved by locals for its constant use of promotional coupons, buffet giveaways, better-than-average odds and an extremely liberal free booze policy, the Lady Luck manages to stay ahead of its Glitter Gulch competitors by catering to serious gamblers and budget-minded seniors.... *Tel 702/477-3000. 206 N. Third St.*

Las Vegas Hilton. How can you not love a place whose split personality lionizes both the King of Rock 'n' Roll and His Ultra-Coolness, 007 (*Casino Royale*, here we come)? The Vegas Hilton may not be the "theme paradise" other Strip casino hotels have become, but there's an intangible sense of weird hipness going on here... something that's bound to get even stranger (and more magnetic) when the $70 million Star Trek Experience opens its doors here in mid-1997. Winner of my ugliest pool in Vegas award for its acres and acres of poured concrete and absence of greenery.... *Tel 702/732–5111. 3000 Paradise Rd.*

Luxor Casino Hotel. If only Tut were alive, he'd be hocking his royal treasures down at the "Largest Pyramid in the World," a mass of glass and steel topped by a beacon visible for hundreds of miles.... *Tel 702/262–4000. 3900 Las Vegas Blvd. S.*

Maxim Casino Hotel. One of Vegas's top comedy clubs is at Maxim, which attracts mostly a low-roller crowd; an amiable place with excellent food at its cafe.... *Tel 702/731–4300. 160 E. Flamingo Rd.*

MGM Grand Casino Hotel and Theme Park. Vegas's largest hotel, with more than 5,000 rooms, MGM is also known as Monty Hall's Nightmare (due to those 5,000 doors); the laundry alone is one of the city's biggest employers! Since it sprawls over an enormous city block, a 10-minute walk from your parked car to one of the three gambling areas is not out of the question. Its cavernous interior is filled with various restaurants, a theme park, a shopping mall, and a few night-clubs.... *Tel 702/891–1111. 3799 Las Vegas Blvd. S.*

Mirage Casino Hotel. An intoxicating, South Pacific environment attracting high rollers from all over the world, as well as Siegfried & Roy's white tigers. Simply elegant, and don't miss the knockout pool area, just your garden-variety rain forest in the desert.... *Tel 702/791–7111. 3400 Las Vegas Blvd. S.*

Monte Carlo Casino Hotel. This impressive new Strip casino hotel has an elegant, James Bond-meets-Mojave design that encompasses miles of blinding whiteness both inside and outside its enormous casino and 3,000-plus rooms. One of the Strip's most outstanding hangouts is Monte Carlo's brewpub, which is so cool it actually attracts young Vegas locals down to the Strip—a rarity!... *Tel 702/730–7777. 3770 Las Vegas Blvd. S.*

New York, New York. Vegas's latest craze consists of visiting this mega-casino hotel and dreaming about what life must be like in the big apple (without having to go). New York, New York transcends the boundaries of East Coast reality and presents instead an encapsulated Manhattan skyline, a huge Statue of Liberty replica, and even shrunken versions of the Brooklyn Bridge and Little Italy.... *Tel 702/740–6969. 3790 Las Vegas Blvd. S.*

Rio Suites Casino Hotel. "Macarena" madness goes Vegas in this glitzy, affable hotel. One of Vegas's hottest nightclubs, a lovely pool area filled with palm trees, cabanas, and lagoons, and the hands-down best buffet in Vegas.... *Tel 702/252–7777. 3700 W. Flamingo Rd.*

Riviera Casino Hotel. The Strip's first high-rise hotel has turned itself into a bawdy, adults-only sort of place that cranks itself up to a frenzied pitch every night of the week.... *Tel 702/734–5110. 2901 Las Vegas Blvd. S.*

CASINOS ⟍ **THE INDEX**

Sam's Town Hotel and Gambling Hall. Sam's Town promotes itself as a local-friendly place, and lives up to the billing with its low prices, cozy scale, comfortable decor, and great reputation for value. Slot players rave about this casino hotel's slot club, which racks up points so fast even a novice player can find himself feasting on comped prime rib after a few sessions. Also the location of the city's best sports bar (see Nightlife).... *Tel 702/456–7777. 5111 Boulder Hwy. (about 5 miles from the Strip).*

Santa Fe Casino Hotel. Earnest attempts at creating a Southwestern appearance have worked to some degree at this North Las Vegas property, which is also home to the city's year-round ice-skating rink, and a 24-hour bowling alley.... *Tel 702/658-4900. 4949 N. Rancho Drive.*

Showboat Casino Hotel. A favorite with locals, the Showboat, with its screwy, N'awlins-meets-Bugsy decor, is most famous for its bowling lanes, which are open 24 hours a day and attract the top touring competitions.... *Tel 702/ 385–9123. 2800 Fremont St.*

Slots-a-Fun. One of the most unhinged places you'll find anywhere, Slots-a-Fun is jammed onto the Strip between Circus Circus (its owner) and the Stardust. It perpetually advertises 75-cent Heinekens, 10-cent slots, and every other sort of low-roller action under the desert sun. This is a great place to come when you're bored, drunk, or in search of some first-rate slumming.... *Tel 702/734–0410. 2880 Las Vegas Blvd. S.*

Stardust Hotel and Casino. This 1,500-room hotel and casino on the Strip manages to balance its ambience between the crass Vegas of yesterday and the ocassionally more sophisticated atmosphere of today. Lots of neon, more than a few low rollers, and a casual, very pleasant atmosphere.... *Tel 702/732–6111. 3000 Las Vegas Blvd. S.*

Stratosphere Casino Hotel. The tallest structure west of Chicago, the 1,149-foot Strat boasts an amusement park, piano bar, and gourmet restaurant. The casino area falls short on ambience, but you've got to come here for the view, if nothing else.... *Tel 702/380–7777. 2000 Las Vegas Blvd. S.*

Treasure Island Casino Hotel. Amazing what a pirate battle staged several times nightly will do for a place's reputation, isn't it? Filled with parents pushing strollers or dragging packs of kids (even after midnight), Treasure Island is also home to Cirque du Soleil, one of Vegas's best shows.... *Tel 702/894–7111. 3300 Las Vegas Blvd. S.*

Tropicana Casino Hotel. It calls itself "The Island of Las Vegas," which sounds corny but trills true in the Trop's very cool jungle decor. Best swimming pool on the Strip, and don't miss the Wildlife Walk (no, we're not referring to the clientele).... *Tel 702/739–2222. 3801 Las Vegas Blvd. S.*

the sho

w scene 2

If your notion of Las Vegas entertainment falls somewhere between Wayne Newton and Nancy Sinatra, prepare for a shock. These days the appeal of this city's main-stage acts isn't totally mired in Vegas's deliriously schlocky past. Yes, you'll still get your fill of comedians, impressionists, magicians, musicians, and, of course, those oh-so-taboo exposed body parts—such acts have always been showroom staples in the City that Never Blinks. But the past several years have seen five decades of stray boa feathers swept up off the stages and replaced with something a lot more striking, a lot louder, probably more expensive than in years past, and—the casinos are hoping—more worth your time and money. At the least, the schlocky past has had an extreme nineties-style face lift.

Though Vegas's reputation was built on headliners like Wayne and Elvis, the big production shows are where most people take their breaks from the tables now. Today's best Las Vegas production shows still build themselves around young, statuesque showgirls and muscled studmuffins (you saw *Showgirls*, didn't you?), but now the performers can actually dance or do gymnastics. The shows are choreographed by seasoned professionals who find it worthwhile to split their careers between Broadway, Hollywood, and Las Vegas; the musical scores are much more hip and current; while the lighting, costuming, and set design keep pace with the industry's latest gadgetry and techno-wizardry. The biggest production shows include Siegfried & Roy, a magic routine using live animals; Cirque du Soleil, a truly unique contemporary circus with acrobats; *EFX*, a Hollywood-style special-effects show; and a Broadway bomb performed on roller skates, retrofitted for the Vegas stage, *Starlight Express*.

If you can't get tickets to see them in the showrooms , you can always catch the stars of these shows leaping out of their private jets parked at McCarran's executive terminal (right on Tropicana behind the San Remo), or driving their Ferraris from their homes in Spanish Trails or Quail Ridge down to the Strip right after rush hour's madness subsides (yes, they too use the access roads behind the casino hotels). Why are they worth millions? Because their shows are sold out two times a night, six nights a week, 40 to 50 weeks a year—at $60 to $80 a head.

A cut below in ticket demand are another dozen or so fast-paced, long-running production spectaculars. These include another magic show *(Spellbound)* several "beautiful men and ladies" revues, some topless, some not *(Jubilee!*, the Rockettes, *Enter the Night*, etc.), impersonator samplers *(Legends in Concert, An Evening at La Cage)*, and theme park–style spectacles *(Splash II*, King Arthur's Tournament). These shows tend to be a bit lower-tech than the biggest spectacles, but the production standards are still high, and you'll probably have an easier time getting tickets for them just because they've been around for awhile.

Despite the rise of the mega-production show, many acts still cater to the tastes of older generations of visitors who have been coming to town for decades and know what they like, as well as to visitors who like their kitsch straight up or of an earlier vintage. Ol' Blue Eyes could still sell out any showroom in the city if he wanted to, as can mighty Wayne and a host of other headliners who've been around since the days of "The Ed Sullivan Show." And if Elvis ever surfaces again, he'll be a lock to at least equal his record-setting string of consecutive sold-out shows (837 at the Las Vegas Hilton, to be exact), playing to the hordes of Japanese honeymooners, German tourists, and beehived American grandmas who can be found elbowing their way through the nickel slots in the back rows of nearly every casino in town. Until then, mere demigods will be counted on to fill the showrooms during "limited engagement" runs. Big-name performers like Bill Cosby, Joan Rivers, Buddy Hackett, Tom Jones, Diana Ross, B.B. King, John Tesh, Alabama, Linda Ronstadt, and Johnny Cash will perpetually light up the neon signs flanking the Strip, showing up for one, two, or maybe as many as 14 evenings of performances.

Sources

To find out which act is playing what showroom for how high a ticket price and at what time of the night, get your hands on a copy of one of the entertainment publications such as *Today in Las Vegas*, *What's On*, or *Showbiz Weekly*, or call the **Las Vegas Convention and Visitors Authority** (tel 702/225–5554) and ask for the latest edition of its "Showguide" pamphlet. All these publications are slickly produced, comprehensive in their listings, and readily available at brochure racks and front desks all over town. The Las Vegas daily newspapers reviews new shows when they open, but don't expect hard-hitting theater criticism; everybody roots for the home team here.

Tickets and Seating

The place you want to sit at most shows is on the second or third level of seats, center stage, which will be roughly at eye level with the performers. For the choicest perches at assigned-seating shows, you simply have to buy your tickets way ahead of time over the phone (call the casino directly). For general-seating performances, you should line up at the showroom entrance at least an hour before the performance. The major production shows tend to be reserved seating, with general seating the rule of thumb below that level. Some of the most popular shows sell "day-of-performance" seats at their box office first thing in the morning, which means you, the nightcrawler, may have to line up with the bright and chipper morning crowd at an hour when you're normally just heading to bed. Weekend tickets are generally harder to find than weekday ones, and, if one of the huge conventions like Comdex is in town, you'll be lucky to get tickets period. Although these shows are now managed nearly as professionally as any big-time theme park, if you get yourself into a tight spot, some showroom maitre d's will still perform a sleight of hand trick worthy of David Copperfield with a proffered $20 bill—yup, that's the minimum going rate or you're gone. And remember: you'll still have to buy a regular-priced seat on top of that, if he lets you in.)

There's no real difference between early and late shows, except at a few of the "beautiful ladies" reviews such as Jubilee! and Follies Bergère, where the dancers will sometimes go topless only in the second show of the night. Ticket prices vary greatly. Some small productions slip under the $20 mark; Siegfried & Roy tix top the field at $83.85. Some prices only get you in the door, some include two drinks and a few even cover dinner, though dinner shows are out of fashion now.

One final tip: Dress as if you've just come in from a day at the beach, and it won't matter how early you get in line for good seats at general admission shows—you won't get in. Use your head. If you don't want to be seated next to the busboy station, leave those Teva sandals in your hotel room and don't even think of wearing shorts or a T-shirt, no matter how super-cool its logo. In Las Vegas, you dress up to watch an elephant disappear.

The Lowdown

The class of the field... The one show here that pleases the critics as well as the crowds is the Treasure Island's **Cirque du Soleil:** *Mystère*. From its music and showmanship to its choreography and breathtaking setting, it's the class act of the Strip. Performed in a 1,542-seat state-of-the-art showroom specially built for this Montreal-based company's perpetually sold-out shows, this surreal two-hour extravaganza features Chinese acrobats, Russian gymnasts, French dancers, Japanese taiko drummers, German trapeze artists—more than 70 performers from 18 countries. You want circus animals? You've come to the wrong place. Cirque du Soleil's idea of a circus is a Dr. Seussian, Roald Dahlian spectacle—acts that use performers' heads as platforms for amazing feats of balance, or trapeze seats rigged to bungee cords that allow a squadron of performers to float high above the audience's heads. Two bits of advice: participate gladly if you're selected from the audience by one of the performers, and don't get pissed off if another performer throws popcorn on you.

Cash acts... Few entertainments left in this world can evoke awe, but Las Vegas is home to at least two that try like crazy. And even if the sight of laser shows and white tigers leaves you cold as entertainment, you may still be awestruck by the amounts of time and money that have gone into these whoppers. Last we checked, **Siegfried & Roy** were the highest-paid entertainers in the history of Las Vegas and the priciest ticket in town. You've seen them in their own TV specials, and enjoyed them on Johnny Carson and Jay Leno. Now that you're in Las Vegas, you may be very sorely tempted to fly right into the flame, and who'd blame you? One way or another—glitzy, amazing, or just plain silly—it's a fun show, smoothly presented, night-in and night-out for nearly 300 nights each year. Presented in a tailor-made, 1,500-seat theater at the Mirage, this megahit can bring out the animal lover in anyone, especially after Roy gallops across the stage on the back of one of the duo's Lexus-sized white tigers—you'll either want to buy a tiger or set all of Siegfried and Roy's troupe free onto the streets of Las Vegas. As smoothly as the show runs, Siegfried and Roy have taken some criticism for appearing to go through the motions on some nights, and both do become much more animated when their tigers are onstage. For 85 bucks, you better hope Siggy and Co. are in a good mood. On the other hand, seeing The Act That Transformed the Strip is as close as any of us are going to get to watching Las Vegas history (whatever that is) in the making. You can't blame the MGM Grand, then, for throwing some magic (and more cash) into *EFX*, the mega–casino hotel's foray into Vegas entertainment, nineties style. The star of *EFX* is acclaimed actor and singer Michael Crawford, who's shed the mask he wore for years in Broadway's *Phantom of the Opera* and instead plays a whole cast of characters, from host to magician (Merlin), to 19th-century futurist writer (H.G. Wells), to escape artist (Houdini). Crawford is overshadowed by the gimmickry as he goes through a roster of standard tricks whipped up, with the help of all the special effects, into illusions that seem more amazing than they are. Another big problem is a weak script that doesn't give its star enough opportunities to do what he does best: sing. Then again, maybe it doesn't matter, given that the music is corny, commercial and blasted at the audience. It sounds more like jingles than show tunes, and it all comes at you at a decibel level somewhere around a jet plane taking off. Another caveat: Avoid the seats way in front—you can gag on the copious fake fog that periodically envelops the proceedings.

Just water, please... Las Vegas producers don't need much of a theme to create a helluva show. Take the Riviera's ***Splash II, Voyage of a Lifetime***, whose star is a 20,000-gallon, glass-sided tank. The whole stage is done up in a submarine ambience and sections of the audience get drenched by waterfalls and other stray spoutings. (If you want to stay dry, do not sit in the front or last row of the lower seating section. And if anyone tries to hand you a raincoat before the show starts—expect precipitation!) The show's specialty performers include a juggler who works at incredible speeds, a surprisingly compelling act which features acrobatic birds, and three trail-bike riders spinning around simultaneously in a 15-foot-tall steel mesh ball. The action flies past at a breakneck pace and everything from the emcee's humor to the set's sound and lights is timed to perfection. Who said vaudeville was dead? It just went swimming.

Merely magical... During the five years **Lance Burton** performed his act at the Hacienda, he billed himself as "Lance Burton: World Champion Magician." He might also have added "...and Vegas's Sexiest Male Star," because his drop-dead good looks have played a not insignificant role in his rise to the short list of the Strip's megastars. Burton is popular enough to have the Monte Carlo's new, 1,200-seat theater named after him, and he keeps it packed five nights a week with his souped-up, spandexed version of the traditional Strip magic show. No, he's not Siegfried & Roy, but then again he's only one man, his show costs less than half as much, and those distractingly tight suits make the sleight of hand that constitutes much of the show all the more surprising. Or maybe more explicable, since a fair amount of the audience seems to be watching anything but his hands. The Harrah's *Spellbound* is another showroom bargain. Performed in a cozy theater that leaves no audience member far from the action, this smooth, straightforward show features magician Mark Kalin, his assistant Jinger (who undergoes so many illusionist near-death experiences you've got to wonder what keeps this woman sane), and a company of well-rehearsed dancers. *Spellbound*'s tricks aren't as mind-boggling as Siegfried & Roy's or even Lance Burton's, just the old-fashioned kinds of escapes patented by the Doug Hennings and David Copperfields of the world. If magic of any kind keeps you spellbound and you want to avoid enormous crowds and high prices, then it's hurray for Harrah's. Otherwise, make yourself disappear.

Broadway West... Perhaps it was inevitable that faded Broadway musicals, like sun-seeking retirees, would turn to Las Vegas to cash in on past investments. Sprung from the same fevered imagination that gave the world *Cats* and *Phantom of the Opera*, **Starlight Express** seems at home in Las Vegas in a way that it surely didn't on Broadway. With the minimal acting, maximum staging, and whiplash you'll get trying to spot a story line amidst all the roller skating, this is more of a production show than a musical. Somehow a romance develops, but it's hard to tell, since half the cast members are padded like hockey goalies (not the ladies, of course), and the sound effects assault your ears like a speeding Union-Pacific locomotive. The score at least rolls, if it doesn't quite rock, and the set is fairly remarkable, designed as it is to accommodate two hours of nonstop roller action on several levels simultaneously. A superior New York import is the Flamingo Hilton's **Forever Plaid**. This squeaky-clean tale of four college glee clubbers who die and perform doo-wop in heaven has its tongue planted deeply in its cheek, and is a refreshing change of pace to stumble across amid the Strip's melange of wired-to-the-max sex and excitement. This is the show to see if you feel queasy sitting next to your parents watching topless dancers do cartwheels. But be warned: if you take the kids, they might need to be woken up occasionally.

Where to take the kids... For whatever reason, you've got the kids along for the evening and you can't just have them at your side at the slot machine, holding your cups of quarters. The best bets to keep them happy are the loud and foggy illusion-fest **EFX**; the loud and silly roller-skating fest *Starlight Express*; the long, white, and tawny animals that make up **Siegfried & Roy**, as well as their tigers; **Lance Burton**'s sleight-of-hand extravaganza; and the **King Arthur's Tournament**, because they can eat with their hands, which may or may not be a novelty in your house.

Best bang for the buck... Clearly, entertainment on the Strip is not usually a budget affair, but at least you deserve to know which ones are really worth what you're paying. On the top of the list, there's **Cirque du Soleil**. It's expensive, but people in Paris and New York pay just as much to see this show. If sheer cheapness matters, **Lance Burton** and *La Cage* offer slick shows for not a lot. An awful lot happens on stage during *Starlight Express*, so if that's your idea of entertainment, you'll be happy. *Country Fever*, *Enter the Night*, and **King Arthur's Tournament** also pack a lot into their shows.

Best show in Glitter Gulch... The big show in downtown Las Vegas is chips flying across tables, not showgirls, and the attitude in this part of town shows it. The area's biggest entertainment is the free **Fremont Experience** (see Hanging Out), a prime example of downtown's screw-you attitude toward the Strip's humongous casino hotels and their big-time entertainment budgets. There is one show here, though, that's worth your time. *Country Fever*, at the Golden nugget Casino and Hotel, packs in locals and tourists six nights a week, earning its reputation as one of the city's best bargains with its swinging choreography, strong country-and-western band (thank God for live musicians!), and unsiliconed dancers. Where else are you gonna catch a gospel-singing act, followed by wicked (but—surprise!—not topless) T&A numbers, followed by a Garth Brooks impersonator? And, for the price of the show, they even throw in a free drink and a basket of deep-fried artery blockers of some sort. The low budget only shows up in the show's kitschy decor, which makes a swipe at looking both Southwestern and contemporary but comes across like Georgia O'Keeffe's worst nightmare. If you want to get your visit to this city off to an affordable, *Viva Las Vegas* beginning, see *Country Fever* on your first night in town.

Best finger food... The vast equestrian arena that's home to **King Arthur's Tournament** is famously short on forks and knives. This, plus the fact that every ticket at the Excalibur Hotel's dinner show comes with a roast Cornish hen, should be warning enough for civilized people. But, of course, kids and other medieval-mannered folks eat this kind of place up. Filled with dirt (take care if you have respiratory problems) and featuring a half-dozen horses charging around at full gallop, the Excalibur's arena is unlike anything else on the Strip. King Arthur calls in the knights for a tourney, and it is their job to please him in order to win the hand of his daughter. There are many two-legged performers in the show, including a wizard, a Galahad, a Launcelot, a Guinevere,

THE SHOW SCENE 〰 THE LOWDOWN

and six knights, not to mention numerous serving wenches with revealing yet still G-rated decolletage, but the horses are the real draw here. Though the horses wear no clothes, the show is intended for a family audience. As to the finger food, the Cornish hen is surprisingly good, as are the corn, broccoli, and biscuit that come with it.

Rich Little on steroids... If you can't see your favorite star when in town, why not see a reasonable facsimile? Between world tours and appearances on "Roseanne" and "Married...With Children," comic/impressionist **Danny Gans** can regularly be caught mimicking more lustrous luminaries at the Stratosphere's 700-seat Broadway Showroom. Contorting both his voice and his Silly Putty face with startling success, he jumps with lightning speed from character to character, morphing through Dr. Ruth, Nat King Cole, Sammy Davis, Jr., Garth Brooks, Willie Nelson, and Bill Clinton, all in the blink of an eye. If you prefer your stars cloned with more reverence, consider *Legends in Concert* at the Imperial Palace. Once the last holdout for the Strip's Elvis-impersonator acts, *Legends in Concert* is, these days, Elvisless. Though Elvis is deeply missed, this show remains worth seeing for the simple reason that the talent know and clearly enjoy what they're doing. Those of you who were unable to see Belushi and Ackroyd do their Blues Brothers routine live and in person will see performers who pull off the act with a flair and polish Jake and Elwood never dreamed possible (and probably never intended), and the Rat Pack themselves (rest their souls) would have a good laugh and another double at the way Sammy Davis, Jr.'s memory is kept very much alive twice nightly. The biggest question you'll have after watching this show is, "How could those performers look so much like the real thing?" To which the only reasonable Las Vegas answer would be to scan the Yellow Pages and start counting the 10 pages' worth of M.D.s listed in the Plastic Surgery section. Still, the fact that Elvis has been shoved aside by the likes of a John Belushi imitator is one of the great unspoken scandals of Las Vegas. It also may say something about changing demographics.

Boys II Women... *An Evening at La Cage* is, as you'd imagine, a drag show inspired by the lovely French film of the early 1980s, *La Cage aux Folles*. Yes, it's men impersonating women right on the stage at the Riviera, a casino hotel fast becoming known as Las Vegas's naughtiest and most unbendingly adult-oriented entertainment mecca. Though drag has gone mainstream in recent years, this down-and-dirty, boys-night-out revue has enough sass in it to curl RuPaul's wig. The show's star is Mr. Frank Marino, who looks damn good in a pair of 5-inch heels; the rest of the cast will at least give you an idea of what Bette Midler would look like if she got a nose job and wore better clothes, and what Aretha Franklin would look like if she thought twice at the buffet table. If you haven't gotten your fill, you can take in the *La Cage* clone, a Las Vegas perennial, ***Boy-Lesque***. There is virtually no difference between the two shows in format and content—and all the guys have great gams. The only curiosity about *Boy-Lesque* is its home. When star performer Kenny Kerr said farewell to the Sahara's Congo Room and took his go-go boots and talented troupe of female impersonators and drag queens over to the Debbie Reynolds Hollywood Hotel/Casino/Museum, even the most jaded of Las Vegas hands did a double-take: talk about an unlikely pairing of sweet cheesecake and wicked beefsteak! *Boy-Lesque* had bounced around the Strip since the late 1970s, but now it looks like the Debbie Reynolds is its home for good. If nothing else, this show's enduring power is a testimony to its producers' single-minded vision—as well as this wacky city's thirst for production shows catering to the more, shall we say, "secretive" side of Las Vegas's conventioneers and family men. Expect to catch your basic Women of Hollywood routines— Streisand, Marilyn, Diana Ross, and Cher, for starters. Oh, and by the way: These girls talk nasty!

Skin shows for a first date... The wholesomest set of prancers in town have got to be the Rockettes. They, of course, never dreamed of dropping their tops when they imported their synchronized, high-stepping dance routines to the Flamingo Hilton Hotel, a devout convert to Las Vegas's family-friendly sect. Here, ***The Great Radio City Spectacular*** plays off the audience's nostalgic yearnings while convincingly affirming that the Rockettes are just a group of nineties gals eager to entertain. The show uses celebrities such as Susan Anton to do its emcee work.

If it has to be topless but it still has to be tasteful, try the Tropicana. The Trop's Tiffany Theatre is not exactly Paris's Right Bank, but it's a more than acceptable substitute setting for the *Folies Bergère*'s two hours of time-tested T&A strutting. Choreographed and directed as a traditional Vegas-style revue, the show harkens back to the past, but isn't constricted by it. *Folies Bergère* is obviously geared toward an older crowd, the sort of Vegas bread-and-butter set who would walk out on anything using music as cutting edge as Devo or the Pretenders in its soundtrack, (and still think this sort of thing a little—blush—naughty). Still, it's hard not to fall in love with the Trop's swanky showroom; you half-expect Ricky Ricardo to jump out from behind the stage's curtains at any moment, banging his congas and blasting the audience with a rip-roaring flash of Miami's South Beach madness. Come to think of it, that just might be a winning theme for this show's needed re-do.

Dirty dancing... Most flashes of flesh on Las Vegas's showroom stages are fairly sanitized by the flood of glitz, so don't get too excited. But a few shows are a notch higher on the sex chart. (To learn your lap-dancing and pole-humping options, consult the Nightlife chapter.) If you've come to town determined to see showgirls prancing around a stage in G-strings and feather headdresses, *Jubilee!* is the show for you—worth seeing simply because it's the furthest evolution of Vegas's traditional form of showroom entertainment. Let's see—beautiful bodies (nearly a hundred of 'em), wrapped around a few outsized production numbers with themes such as Samson and Delilah or the sinking of the Titanic. Depending on your frame of reference, you might find Bally's spectacular a shade on the cornpone side, but that's the beauty of it. Everything that happens on the *Jubilee!* stage is intended to be taken with a grain of salt. The show's dance numbers are all elegantly choreographed, and its costumers are among the best in town. It's a good bet if you're in a swanky mood, so order a Tom Collins and enjoy. Women looking for some entertainment geared toward their own prurient interests might prefer the Stardust's more contemporary revue, *Enter the Night*, in which the ubiquitous topless showgirls are counterbalanced by pelvis-swinging, body-building male dancers. Performed in a cozy showroom that echoes Vegas's past while bowing to its high-tech present (the place has been renovated with top-notch lighting and sound systems), this show and its acrobatic performers rock from start to finish—and the casino even throws in a couple of freebie drinks to keep your brains scrambled. If the drinks don't confuse you, the specialty acts will: Two ice skaters perform a daredevil routine on a tiny rink, and then Los Huincas Gauchos, an updating of traditional Argentinean rodeo entertainment, throw knives, bowling pins, and other Argentinian paraphenalia such as the *pelota* at each other. For more unadulterated adult-oriented showgirl fare, the Riv's all-female *Crazy Girls* is a non-stop, comedy-laced T&A spectacular. Wow! If "Benny Hill" meets *Oh! Calcutta!* sounds like a great evening to you, step right up. They get straight to the point here—no frills, no big build-up. Bring a date, and the back seat of your rental car might look as appealing as it did when you were 16.

Clean dancing... If you've ever had the urge to dress up like Carmen Miranda, you're gonna love *Copacabana*, a colorful dinner show at the Rio that culminates in a seat-clearing conga line. On the other hand, if you tire easily from fairly standard dance routines and have a low tolerance for mild, slapstick comedy numbers, *Copacabana* will probably try your patience. Performed in a theater/nightclub that does double duty as one of Vegas's hottest places to dance after midnight, this well-staged show is calculated to appeal to the early dinner crowd from Spokane—so it lacks a certain edge that works well in other showrooms. However, it's one of the few remaining dinner shows in town; in fact, the dance numbers are inspired by the menu—twirling radishes, garlic-chopping chefs, a salad bowl that emerges from the depths below the dance floor (the costumes are the best part of the night). The whole stage show is accompanied by a booming PA system and a bank of video images that normally serve Club Rio, the dressy, wild dance party that takes over the room every night when the clock strikes midnight.

Where the headliners are... Though a little overshadowed by the big shows right now, the headliners are where second- and third- and fortieth-time visitors to Vegas go once they've seen the illusions and the tiger tricks. In general, a headliner show is a muscled-up version of what you might see when that star tours, drawing on the wealth of available dancers and production talent this city offers. Each casino hotel books its headliners in keeping with the demographics of its bread-and-butter clientele. The Las Vegas Hilton, Bally's, Tropicana, MGM Grand, Desert Inn, Mirage, and Caesar's Palace only book the occasional rocker—these are the places where you'll find Neil Diamond, Linda Ronstadt, and other such VH-1, lite-music types. On the other end, Aladdin and the Hard Rock are competitive when it comes to booking headliner rock, blues, and alternative bands. Debbie's Star Theater at the Debbie Reynolds Hollywood Hotel/Casino/Museum is home to the eternally chipper screen star and her fifties film- and recording-star pals. There's more nostalgia on tap in the similarly intimate Desert Inn Crystal Room, where Tony Bennett, Steve and Eydie, and the Everly Brothers still croon away to swooning forty- and fiftysomethings, and the Sands Copa Showroom, where you'll find Sid Caesar or Wayne Newton. Several showrooms (Bally's, Caesars Palace Circus Maximus, Riviera, Desert Inn, Tropicana) continue to book headliner comedians, but the audience for big-name comics appears to have peaked during the Great Comic Glut of the 1980s. On the other hand, though there are far fewer comedians playing Vegas these days, when they're here, they're worth seeing: Bill Cosby, Joan Rivers, Dennis Miller, and Don Rickles all have reputations for putting on memorable shows in Las Vegas, just as Buddy Hackett has a reputation for putting on crude ones. You'll be sorry if you pass up a chance to see Johnny Cash; the same goes for Tom Jones. And the word is you won't be sorry if you pass on Barbara Mandrell or Linda Ronstadt.

The Index

Boy-Lesque. This wicked (but tastefully done, of course) drag show sets up shop these days in the unlikely setting of the Debbie Reynolds Hollywood Hotel/Casino/Museum, drawing a raucous crowd of gays and straights as well as bouffant Midwestern gals.... *Tel 702/733–2243. Debbie Reynolds Hollywood Hotel/Casino/Museum, Star Theatre, 305 Convention Center Dr. Shows Mon–Fri 10:30; Sat 9:00. Admission $24.95.*

Cirque du Soleil: *Mystère*. An entertainment experience unlike anything else you'll see in Las Vegas. Especially powerful because the company performs in its own custom-designed, state-of-the-art performance space inside the Treasure Island.... *Tel 702/894–7111. Treasure Island Casino Hotel, Cirque du Soleil Showroom, 3300 Las Vegas Blvd. S. Shows Wed–Sun 7:30 and 10:30. Admission $59.95 (adults), $29.95 (kids).*

Copacabana. A mildly humorous dinner show that's short on cheesecake but long on choreography, *Copacabana* is fun kitsch. Staged in a state-of-the-art nightclub that's loaded with all the latest video, lighting, and sound goodies.... *Tel 702/252–7777. Rio Suites Casino/Hotel, Copacabana Room, 3700 W. Flamingo Rd. Shows Tues–Sat 6:00 and 8:30. Admission $51.75 (includes dinner).*

Country Fever. This intense, well-designed show may sound like an iffy proposition for a Vegas production show, but it works because of its rock-solid professionalism, from the dancers to the choreography to the production values. And, its Glitter Gulch's only stage show worth going to.... *Tel 702/386–8100. Golden Nugget Casino Hotel, Cabaret Theatre, 129 E. Fremont St. Shows Mon–Thur, Sat–Sun 7:15 and 9:45. Admission $22.50.*

Crazy Girls. Vegas topless revues are a bread-and-butter commodity, and *Crazy Girls* fits right into the mold with this rocked-out, late-night T&A fest.... *Tel 702/794–9433. Riviera Casino Hotel, Mardi Gras Plaza, 2901 Las Vegas Blvd. S. Shows Tue–Sun 8:30 and 10:30; late show Fri–Sat midnight. Admission $16.95.*

Danny Gans: The Man of Many Voices. Vegas used to be loaded with impressionists, but today there's only one world-class pro working who can pack a house night-in, night-out. Danny Gans works with a live rock band, lots of charm, and boundless energy in covering anyone from Madonna to Jay Leno.... *Tel 702/380–7711. Stratosphere Casino Hotel, Broadway Showroom, 2000 Las Vegas Blvd. S. Shows Mon, Thur–Sun 9:00. Admission $29.50 (includes two drinks).*

EFX. This glitzy, over-the-top display of special-effects pyrotechnics stars Michael Crawford (a.k.a. the Phantom of the Opera), who performs illusionist and magic routines using wild costumes, props, hydraulic lifts, sound effects, and anything else they can think of to make this a "spectacle." The evening's show is wrapped around a narrative having to do with a journey through time and space, but the title says it all.... *Tel 702/891–7777. MGM Grand Casino Hotel, Grand Theatre, 3900 Las Vegas Blvd. S. Shows Mon–Wed, Fri–Sat 7:30 and 10:30; Sun 7:30. Admission $70 for adults, $35 for kids.*

Enter the Night. This very modern version of the traditional Vegas production show has lots of topless women and well-muscled men in wonderful costumes, interspersed with amusing speciality acts, all offered in the Stardust's intimate theater.... *Tel 702/732–6111. Stardust Casino Hotel, Stardust Theatre, 3000 Las Vegas Blvd. S. Shows Tue–Thur, Sat 7:30 and 10:30; Sun–Mon 8:00. Admission $26.90.*

An Evening at La Cage. Men in 5-inch heels may not be your idea of an evening's fun, but this combination of outrageous attitudes, Vegas production-show staging and the most flamboyant costuming imaginable will entertain even the most skeptical.... *Tel 702/794–9433. Riviera Casino Hotel, Mardi Gras Plaza, 2901 Las Vegas Blvd. S. Shows*

Mon–Sun 7:30 and 9:30; late show Wed and Sat 11:15. Admission $18.95.

Folies Bergère. In one form or another, *Folies Bergère* Vegas-style has been around since 1961. At times, the show's choreography makes what the dancers are doing onstage look outdated and silly (if not boring), but its a favorite show of Vegas's older visitor, and will probably be around long after the rest of us have been locked away.... *Tel 702/739–2411. Tropicana Casino Hotel, Tiffany Theatre, 3801 Las Vegas Blvd. S. Shows Mon–Fri, Sun 7:30 and 10:30. 7:30 dinner show, $30.95; 10:30 cocktail show, $23.95.*

Forever Plaid. Sweetness and harmless fun may seem better suited to places other than the Vegas Strip, but *Forever Plaid* is a very popular show that proves just who and where this city's "new breed" of tourist is coming from. Just a good time, and suitable for families with children past the squirmiest stage.... *Tel 702/733–3333. Flamingo Hilton Casino Hotel, Bugsy's Celebrity Theatre, 3555 Las Vegas Blvd. S. Shows Tue–Sun 7:30 and 10:00. Admission $19.95.*

The Great Radio City Spectacular. A nostalgic, energetic show, beautifully choreographed and sure to bring some Rockefeller-Center, Macy's-at-Christmas images to mind.... *Tel 702/733–3333. Flamingo Hilton Casino/Hotel, Flamingo Hilton Showroom, 3555 Las Vegas Blvd. S. Shows Mon–Thur, Sat–Sun 7:45 and 10:30. 7:45 dinner show, $55; 10:30 cocktail show, Admission $38.20.*

Jubilee! Las Vegas was once filled to the rafters with the sort of fan-dancer/showgirl stage acts known as "feather shows," and in a way, *Jubilee!* is the last of the lot. However, this is a very professionally done version of a feather show, one where the dancers have old-fashioned, towering (and probably very heavy) headdresses and G-strings, accompanied by smooth-as-silk contemporary production values.... *Tel 702/739–4567. Bally's Casino Hotel, Jubilee Theatre, 3645 Las Vegas Blvd. S. Shows Tue–Thur, Sat 8:00 and 11:00; Sun–Mon 8:00. Admission $46.00.*

King Arthur's Tournament. Another family show, this one combines an inexpensive and surprisingly good dinner that you eat without utensils (sorta Prince Valiant–style) with a jousting tourney among six equestrian knights vying for the hand of King Arthur's daughter. If you like horses or roast Cornish game hen, you'll have fun.... *Tel 702/597–7600. Excalibur Casino Hotel, King Arthur's Arena, 3850 Las Vegas Blvd. S. Shows nightly 6:00 and 8:30. Admission $29.95.*

Lance Burton: Master Magician. A very popular Vegas performer whose good looks are eclipsed only by the speed of his sleight-of-hand routines, Lance Burton performs in the Strip's newest performance hall, a 1,200-seat palace configured like a legitimate theater.... *Tel 702/730–7000. Monte Carlo Casino Hotel, Lance Burton Theatre, 3770 Las Vegas Blvd. S. Shows Tue–Sat 7:30 and 10:30. Admission $34.95.*

Legends in Concert. Although the Elvis impersonator is gone, you can still expect lots of eerily great routines, and a plastic surgeon's field of look-alike dreams.... *Tel 702/794–3261. Imperial Palace Casino Hotel, Imperial Theatre, 3535 Las Vegas Blvd. S. Shows Mon–Sat 7:30 and 10:30. Admission $29.95.*

Siegfried & Roy. The most popular entertainers on the Strip have performed worldwide with their magic and white tiger routines. If you're here for the first time, you've got to see Siegfried & Roy. They're Vegas's version of the Empire State Building.... *Tel 702/792–7777. Mirage Casino Hotel, Siegfried & Roy Theatre, 3400 Las Vegas Blvd. S. Shows Mon–Tue, Thur–Sun 7:30 and 11:00. Admission $83.85.*

Spellbound. A sophisticated magic show that tends to use all the other state-of-the-art magic tricks being employed elsewhere in the Strip's production shows, *Spellbound* is worth seeing if you haven't already had your fill of magic acts.... *Tel 702/369–5222. Harrah's Casino Hotel, Commander's Theatre, 3475 Las Vegas Blvd. S. Shows Mon–Sat 7:30 and 10:00. Admission $29.95.*

Splash II, Voyage of a Lifetime. This production show takes place at blinding speed, with lots of laughs and megawatts of energy. Good sets, great fun, lots of flesh, and a refreshing tendency to laugh at itself.... *Tel 702/477–5274. Riviera*

Casino Hotel, Splash Theatre, 2901 Las Vegas Blvd. S. Shows nightly 7:30 and 10:30. Admission $39.95.

Starlight Express. A hit in London but a flop on Broadway, this Andrew Lloyd Webber show proves right up Vegas's alley: fast-paced, middle-brow entertainment that doesn't require too much attention from the audience. The actors stay on their skates, doing their roller thing at blinding speed.... *Tel 702/732–5755. Las Vegas Hilton, Las Vegas Hilton Showroom, 3000 Paradise Rd. Shows Tue–Thur, Sat–Sun 7:30 and 10:30; Mon, Wed 7:30. Admission $19.50–$45.00.*

nigh

tlife 3

From techno-discos with FX wizardry rivaling Industrial Light and Magic's, to romantic nooks, to T&A joints that make *Showgirls* look tame by comparison,

Vegas's nightlife caters to the needs of *every* variety of night-crawler. Much of the action occurs at the hotel bars and lounges. The human ear can only take the relentless sound of a slot machine's "ka-ching, ka-ching" for so long, so nearly every one of the city's casinos has at least one lounge featuring live music. These offer everything from Gershwin to grunge. Las Vegas has almost single-handedly kept that oh-so-fifties term "lounge" in Webster's. And lounge is exactly what people do: They sprawl here in between casino splurges, shopping sprees, and buffet spreads. With a few notable exceptions, the largest, most extravagant dance clubs are usually attached to the hotels as well. So are the stand-up venues. About the only thing you won't find is bump-and-grind.

In general, a casino's main lounge either opens up to the middle of its gambling area (Las Vegas Hilton, Stratosphere, Riviera) or is tucked just off the casino's high-traffic zone... out of players' earshot, yet close enough for anyone to reach in a minute or two (Caesars Palace, MGM Grand). If your tastes run toward either the very loud or very soft end of the musical spectrum, steer clear. Vegas lounge bands, though versatile, play music targeted toward pleasing a diverse audience. This means "Summer in the City" is made to sound like "A Summer Place," while "Party Doll" comes out more like "You've Got to Fight for the Right to Party."

This action takes place all night long, thanks to Nevada's legendarily loose liquor laws, which allow booze to flow 24 hours a day—and explain why, on weekends, nobody around here seems in much of a hurry to get anywhere until after midnight. Closing hours, where they exist, are a loosely held concept at best, and you'll find most lounges, clubs and nightspots keeping their doors open way into the morning hours, provided there's a crowd on hand. Even on weeknights, most of these joints don't start jumping until 10pm, with the scene shifting from place to place depending on which clubs are running what sort of crowd-magnetizing specials (tie-ins with radio stations or liquor companies, usually), or which clubs have booked the hottest dance/touring bands. Las Vegas locals are acclimated to their own version of *The Late Shift*, which is why parking lots outside many places stay packed until dawn.

Folks who finally pry themselves away from whatever slot machine they've been chained to for six hours needn't worry when they venture forth for a drink. Besides the club scene's social appeal there's also gambling action—any bar in Vegas can get licensed for 10 slot machines, and most clubs in the city have video-poker slots recessed into their bars. A video screen stares at you from the exact spot where you'd normally place your drink, encouraging dozens of deadpan Nicolas Cage wannabes, all reflected in the machines' glassy exteriors, to kill two birds with one stone. What do you expect in a town whose swim-up bars often double as floating craps games or blackjack tables?

Getting Past the Velvet Rope

In a town where they virtually give away prime rib, don't look for the intimidating gate attendants you might be accustomed to in bigger cities. When live music is on tap, most nightclubs and bars charge either a cover or a two-drink minimum (the minimum is much more common in casino lounges). Covers range from a few bucks at a blues bar to 10 dollars at one of Las Vegas's more popular dance clubs. The exception is when an out-of-town touring band is booked for a one-night stand; then the covers jump to $15 and $20. Alcohol is not allowed at clubs featuring totally nude dancers, except for the Palomino, which is in North Las Vegas and was grandfathered into Clark County's ban, so if you're heading out to those places, expect to pay $7 for a Snapple. If you want a cold beer with your lap dance, you'll have to stick to places like Cheetahs, the Olympic Garden, and other topless clubs.

What To Wear

The friendliness/dressiness/crowdedness varies from club to club, depending on the kind of music played and the clientele the place attracts. A useful rule of thumb for casino lounges is that the acts tend to be surprisingly polished and the crowds manicured accordingly; jackets usually go over well—but you don't need a tie. There are also several Vegas nightclubs—for instance, The Drink, The Nightclub, and Club Rio—where you'll definitely want to wear those linen and silk numbers hanging in your closet (dress codes are common—you'll be turned away at the door if you show up looking like you've been gardening all day). Then there are the "underground" clubs where no dress code is enforced, but the 'tude is fierce if you don't boast multiple tattoos and piercings. Fortunately, even if you're not in trendy mode, a relaxed, casual atmosphere prevails at most bars and clubs, with shorts and a T-shirt as the bare necessities.

Nightlife Near The Strip and Paradise Road

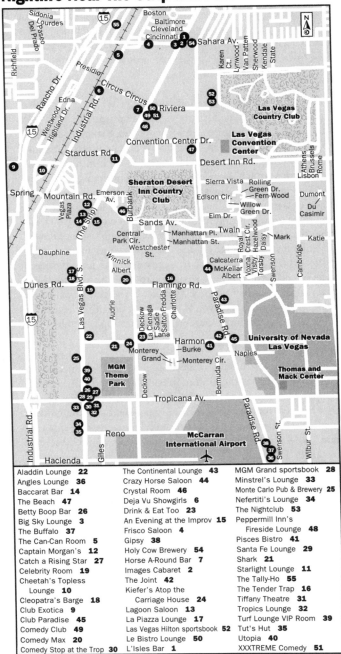

Aladdin Lounge **22**	The Continental Lounge **43**	MGM Grand sportsbook **28**
Angles Lounge **36**	Crazy Horse Saloon **44**	Minstrel's Lounge **33**
Baccarat Bar **14**	Crystal Room **46**	Monte Carlo Pub & Brewery **25**
The Beach **47**	Deja Vu Showgirls **6**	Nefertiti's Lounge **34**
Betty Boop Bar **26**	Drink & Eat Too **23**	The Nightclub **53**
Big Sky Lounge **3**	An Evening at the Improv **15**	Peppermill Inn's
The Buffalo **37**	Frisco Saloon **4**	Fireside Lounge **48**
The Can-Can Room **5**	Gipsy **38**	Pisces Bistro **41**
Captain Morgan's **12**	Holy Cow Brewery **54**	Santa Fe Lounge **29**
Catch a Rising Star **27**	Horse A-Round Bar **7**	Shark **21**
Celebrity Room **19**	Images Cabaret **2**	Starlight Lounge **11**
Cheetah's Topless	The Joint **38**	Tut's Hut **35**
Lounge **10**	Kiefer's Atop the	The Tally-Ho **55**
Cleopatra's Barge **18**	Carriage House **24**	The Tender Trap **16**
Club Exotica **9**	Lagoon Saloon **13**	Tiffany Theatre **31**
Club Paradise **45**	La Piazza Lounge **17**	Tropics Lounge **32**
Comedy Club **49**	Las Vegas Hilton sportsbook **52**	Turf Lounge VIP Room **39**
Comedy Max **20**	Le Bistro Lounge **50**	Tut's Hut **35**
Comedy Stop at the Trop **30**	L'Isles Bar **1**	Utopia **40**
		XXXTREME Comedy **51**

Las Vegas Area Nightlife

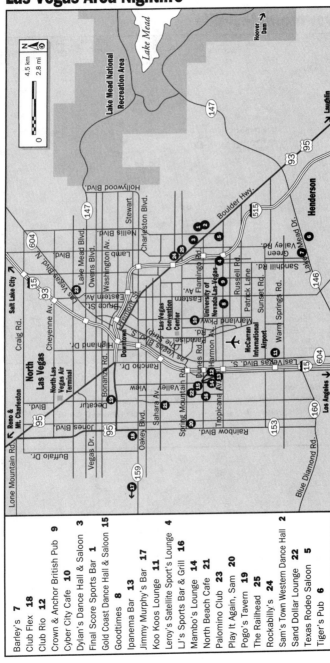

Barley's **7**
Club Flex **18**
Club Rio **12**
Crown & Anchor British Pub **9**
Cyber City Cafe **10**
Dylan's Dance Hall & Saloon **3**
Final Score Sports Bar **1**
Gold Coast Dance Hall & Saloon **15**
Goodtimes **8**
Ipanema Bar **13**
Jimmy Murphy's Bar **17**
Koo Koos Lounge **11**
Leroy's Satellite Sport's Lounge **4**
LJ's Sports Bar & Grill **16**
Mambo's Lounge **14**
North Beach Cafe **21**
Palomino Club **23**
Play It Again, Sam **20**
Pogo's Tavern **19**
The Railhead **25**
Rockabilly's **24**
Sam's Town Western Dance Hall **2**
Sand Dollar Lounge **22**
Texas Rodeo Saloon **5**
Tiger's Pub **6**

Downtown Nightlife

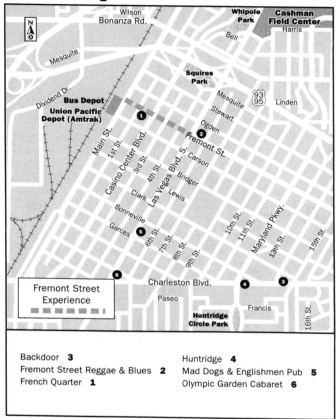

Backdoor **3**

Fremont Street Reggae & Blues **2**

French Quarter **1**

Huntridge **4**

Mad Dogs & Englishmen Pub **5**

Olympic Garden Cabaret **6**

The Lowdown

Best gawking... The crowd at the Rio Suites' **Club Rio** is always fashionable, and this is never more obvious than during Latin-themed nights—when it's a toss-up as to which clings more, the dresses or the ladies' boyfriends—and Wednesday's disco night, when you'll actually see Travolta-style white polyester suits and the occasional Disco Diva drag queen sashaying about, lip-synching a Sylvester song. Thursdays at **Goodtimes** are Trash Disco nights, when up-and-coming drag princesses mingle with the leather-and-Levis crowd, including dykes on bikes. **Jimmy Murphy's Bar** sounds like a homey Irish pub, and they may serve Guinness, but only the stout-of-heart should venture into this pit where mohawked dudes and dudettes butt heads on the dance floor, and there are enough body piercings to lend new meaning to the term "chain gang." Anyone and everyone seems to fit in at **Utopia**, a place filled with strange people of all genders and sexual preferences who probably don't want to talk to you, but who definitely want you to ooh and aah over their torn clothes, body modifications (you can have your nose pierced right next to the bar, if you're in that sort of mood), and hip-hopper-than-thou attitudes. You'll find everything from Harleys to Bentleys parked outside the **Sand Dollar Lounge**, Vegas's hottest blues bar, with a discerning clientele to match. Black predominates, whether leather jackets or tuxedos. And at the **Cyber City Cafe**, a conglomeration of cyber-geeks, from low-level execs to students in jeans and T-shirts, squint at monitors while wired on high-test java.

Theme drinking... The Tropicana's **Tropics Lounge** has one of the Strip's wildest environments. It's jungle time here, with squawking, exotic caged birds, and youngish singles who practically swing from the rafters. While the Excalibur's medieval environment, buxom serving wenches and all, is a little on the disorienting side (did they really drink kamikazes in the 10th century?), its **Minstrel's Lounge** tends to book some of the best dance bands in the city. Leave the armor at home. **Cleopatra's Barge** at Caesars Palace is an actual floating bar (Caesars had to fence off its indoor pond to prevent drunks from falling beneath the barge's gangplank). It's spacious enough for a stage, a dance floor, and a few hundred in the audience. If you've sunk so low, you're welcome to fondle the wooden breasts of the sea nymph carved into the barge's prow; from their perfect gloss it's apparent many have succumbed to the temptation. The Luxor chimes in with its own ancient chic, **Tut's Hut**. This is actually (go figure) a Polynesian pub, replete with bamboo columns and gargantuan Day-Glo drinks topped with fruit and umbrellas. What any of this has to do with Egypt is anyone's guess. If you prefer a more classic Egyptian experience, there's always the Luxor's **Nefertiti's Lounge**, (recently expanded) sitting on the banks of their faux Nile—Yul Brynner and Anne Baxter never had it so good. If you're not in a *Ten Commandments* kind of mood, **Play it Again, Sam**'s re-creates the set of *Casablanca*, with plenty of sweaty, beefy types standing in for Sydney Greenstreet. **Horse A-Round Bar** at Circus Circus would be the perfect place to take the kids if it weren't a hard-core drinking establishment: The entire room is decked out like a carousel, complete with gaudy horsey seats. Thankfully, it doesn't revolve—and you're spared the calliope music. The Mirage's **Lagoon Saloon** perches in the middle of the hotel's rainforest atrium. You sit in parrot-themed chairs under a bougainvillea arbor amid waterfalls and lagoons; you're serenaded by trills, caws, and a lite musical menu ranging from pop to Porter; and the bar top duplicates a sandy beach—it even has shells.

Night fever, night fever... Wednesday night at **Club Rio** belongs to the Boogie Knights, a seventies-music revival group with Afro wigs, bell-bottoms, platform shoes, and a musical repertoire covering K.C. and the Sunshine Band, Barry White, the Commodores, etc. This is a great place to wear those hip-huggers or that green vinyl dress. **Goodtimes** throws an even wilder disco nightmare catering primarily to the gay set and the straights who love them. The fashion (non)sense and steady diet of Donna Summer are enough to make anyone wax nostalgic.

For Marlboro men—and women... **Dylan's Dance Hall and Saloon** finds the real McCoys (and Hatfields) two-stepping in full gallop or lassoing each other at the bar. **Sam's Town Western Dance Hall** tends to attract a more touristy crowd—the kind that buys their ten-gallon hats at Neiman Marcus, and who don't scuff their Ferragamos and Fryes. **Rockabilly's** is generally considered to have the best bands, line dancers, and good-natured lessons for first-timers. It's a gay old time at the **Texas Rodeo Saloon**, the top country/western same-sex hangout, where leather chaps reign on Underwear Night. **Gold Coast Dance Hall and Saloon** caters to more mature urban cowfolk, who two-step gracefully around the gigantic oval dance floor almost as large as a trailer park.

Going hog wild... **Sand Dollar Lounge** has a well-deserved reputation for being one of Vegas's leading biker hangouts—the kind of place where half the guys in the crowd look as if they're itching for a fight. This isn't the kind of joint where you want to get into a staring contest with some drunk across the bar. On the other hand, the live blues sets are even meaner, so it's worth a stop. **The Buffalo** is its gay equivalent, though much cozier and down home; the attire may be leather/Levis/chains, but it's mostly posing, nothing hard core.

One, two, cha-cha-cha... For a strong whiff of salsa and merengue rhythms, check out the Rio Suites' **Mambo's Lounge**, where the dance bands really do have an authentic Latin flavor—though in typical Vegas fashion, the decor is ersatz Trader Vic's, with thatched roofing, rice-paper fans, and bamboo furnishings. Or you can mambo over to the Rio's **Ipanema Bar**, where the waitresses are all done up as *girls* from Ipanema (sans accent) and libations run toward Copa Bananas (rum, banana liqueur, blackberry brandy). **Fremont Street Reggae & Blues** is predictably heavy on ska, reggae, and soca, but occasionally books super salsa, merengue, and beguine acts. The clien-

NIGHTLIFE ⟨ **THE LOWDOWN**

tele and decor are equally colorful; the latter features walls in Rasta yellow, green, and red.

Where even the locals go... The Strip's most popular lounge is **The Nightclub**, a two-story lair inside the Las Vegas Hilton, whose house band, Kristine W. and the Sting, has scored more than one hit song on *Billboard* magazine's Club Play charts. The muted, James Bond-ish atmosphere perfectly fits Ms. Kristine's techno-synth music and young–Liz Taylor looks. **Club Rio** is an equally luxe lounge, wildly popular both for theme nights (e.g. disco, Latin) and for dance bands that specialize in covering what's hot right now. **The Joint** at the Hard Rock Hotel also attracts an oh-so-cool crowd, despite—or maybe because of—the fact that this particular lounge is open only while live music rocks the house. The Joint features touring national acts (everything from Chris Isaak to the Reggae Sunsplash tour) that generally take to the stage around 9 or 10pm, which means this place is open only for a few hours (at best). **The Railhead**, at Boulder Station Casino Hotel, is located on the Boulder Highway, about 5 miles away from the Strip—a corner of Las Vegas nicknamed the Boulder Strip (its many casino hotels, including Sam's Town, cater primarily to a home-town crowd). Locals appreciate The Railhead as much for the lack of tourists as for its fantastic booking agent, who corrals acts as diverse as the Coasters and Clarence Clemons. On evenings when the Aladdin has a big-name rock band in its showroom, its **Aladdin Lounge** turns into one of Vegas's places to be, usually with a rockin' house act that plays until 5am or so.

Where the locals don't go... Stratosphere, a new casino hotel at the north end of the Strip, has the **L'Isles Bar**, a Jimmy Buffett-y, Caribbean-lite kind of place which books good local acts, and **Images Cabaret**, a more serious dance place (once the impressionist leaves, that is). L'Isles has that island thing going for it, but Images has the same problem as the rest of the Stratosphere—cold, impersonal decor which leaves visitors feeling a bit lost. So far, Vegas residents are staying away from the Strat in droves, feeling that it's not friendly to locals, so you'll be hanging with hotel guests if you come here. For a taste of the old days, check out the Stardust for its retro-Vegas appeal and pink neon, not to mention the Midwesterners and ranchers crowding around the gambling tables before repairing to the **Starlight Lounge**, a place that often jumps until dawn, but usually not with locals; the Stardust is a little too nostalgia-driven for those who are tired of *Ocean's Eleven* jokes and winking Rat Pack references.

Cozy nooks... When you're not barging down the Nile, Caesars also has the **La Piazza Lounge**, a more laid-back environment where the emphasis isn't so much on dancing as it is on soaking up the Piazza's sleek, European atmosphere and polished lounge acts. Everything at **Kiefer's Atop the Carriage House** is geared toward a romantic evening out, from the frosted candle lamps to the glittering tiara of the Strip viewed from vaulting picture windows: It's the kind of place to propose or let someone down easy. The ambience at **Peppermill Inn's Fireside Lounge** is as warm as the name suggests, with sumptuous circular sofas, potted and hanging plants strategically placed to isolate seating areas, and a gas fireplace whose licks of flame are cleverly reflected in a shimmering pool. **Pisces Bistro**, at the tony all-suites Alexis Park (which offers discreet digs for celebs like Alan Alda, Alec Baldwin, Whitney Houston, and Robert DeNiro), is one of the more opulent nightspots in Vegas, with a 30-foot domed ceiling crossed with rough-hewn beams, greenery tumbling voluptuously over the tiered balconies like a latter-day Hanging Gardens of Babylon, and classy vocalists and combos playing show tunes and pop standards at just the right level. Hidden away amongst its range of environments, **Drink & Eat Too** (a k a "the Drink") features that latest craze, a quiet corner bar, complete with expensive cigars, single malts, brandies, and gentlemen pontificating on all of the above.

Most upscale... The **Nightclub**'s cushy art deco style is updated by such high-tech tricks as etched glass panels lit with shifting colors. The plush **Club Rio** is the spot for yuppies who want to practice their Arthur Murray lessons to everything from samba to salsa, then segue into their usual jerky, white-boy flailing. **Drink & Eat Too**'s atmosphere is more seventies/hipster, with psychedelic colors splashed across the arty techno digs (lots of exposed pipes for that once-hip SoHo warehouse look), but the clientele is strictly yupster, with cell phones slung like pistols at the hips and guys comparing the length and thickness of their stogies like giggling teenage boys.

Meet markets... When not-so-sweet young things want romance of a more transient nature, they head for **The Beach**. The barely legal crowd here is definitely not interested in dressing up. You'll see lots of muscle Ts, cutoffs, and halter tops, the better to display the wares. The Beach offers a night of dancing to wild, thumping music and a crowd so primed to party you wonder how much longer they're going to keep their clothing on. Clothes, in fact, are optional inside—employees of both sexes wear skimpy bathing suits, and dozens of paying customers seem compelled to rip off their shirts and start dancing on top of the bars. Such behavior is encouraged. The clientele at **Mad Dogs and Englishmen** is just that; if Cockney, Aussie, or Kiwi accents (and punk-rock chic) turn you on, then you'll enjoy elbowing Sid Vicious and Courtney Love types at the bar or on the postage-stamp-sized dance floor. Beware: On weekends, the low ceilings exacerbate the loud bar talk, louder tuneless bands, and cig fumes. **The Shark** (piranha might be more like it) becomes a feeding frenzy as the night wears on, attracting men and women traveling in their respective packs, eyeing prospects over their drinks as they prepare to make a move. The two ground-floor bars in the back of **The Joint**, along with its balcony bar, are not as much of a meet market, but are still a good place to score (unless you're here just to enjoy the music—buy a standing-room ticket and you'll save a few bucks, too). Believe it or not, **Cyber City Cafe** is one of the hottest pickup joints in town. You can sign online to pick someone up in cyber-space, or demurely ask the hacker next to you how to log on. Vegas has been lining up at **the Drink** since mid-1995 thanks to its slyly horny singles atmosphere: It comes up aces in come-ons for the somewhat dressy 25-to-45 age group, who groove to the beat, the mod-colored flowers gracing the rough-textured walls and mini-malist-cool exposed ducts.

Tickling the ivories... You can easily let time go by at **Play It Again, Sam**, where the pianist offers jazz and "easy listening" to a local crowd, and even the video slots are conveniently muffled to maximize conversation. **Kiefer's** is downright dangerous. As the silky pianist glides through an amazing repertoire, the lights of the Strip twinkle bewitchingly, and before you know it you might be saying "I do" in a cheesy chapel down the block. Treasure Island's **Captain Morgan's** boasts elaborate entrance arches and gilded skull-and-crossbones chandeliers—actual plaster casts of scapulas, femurs, and the like, by the way—to distract you from the pianist du jour. The **Baccarat Bar** at the Mirage is, depending on your take, either suave or snooty, with jacket and tie required for men (well, after all, does anyone really play baccarat other than James Bond?). With that kind of dress code (and high tippers), the pianist gladly, even soulfully plays requests for "Melancholy Baby" and "Sunny."

For those who only wear black... If you wear your hair long and stringy like a metal-head, stop off at the deceptively bland-on-the-outside **Frisco Saloon**, where you'll find Lycra is a preferred fashion statement for the women, and combat boots and fatigues standard attire for the guys (or is it the other way around?). The most underground of Vegas's bands make **Jimmy Murphy's Bar**, a Westside hangout, their adopted home. Don't even *think* of wearing anything but black, be sure to bring your ID, polish up your navel ring, don't leave anything valuable on the front seat of your car... and you'll have a great time with all the other 25-year-olds writhing in front of the stage.

Toga parties... No, we're not talking Caesars Palace again. A frat-house atmosphere prevails at **The Beach**; indeed, stationed right by each of its two entrances are huge, galvanized steel tubs loaded with shaved ice and longneck bottles of brew... along with "a babe" in a thong bikini who asks you some variation of "Hey dude, wanna cold one?" It's a living beer commercial.

For thirtysomethings... **The Nightclub** is the most intimate disco in town, with an elegant art deco cityscape mural and a quieter balcony with a fine view of the band and dancers. **The Shark** is Vegas's one true ethnic melting pot, reflected by the music—mostly techno pop and hip-hop. Though it sees more than its share of barely legals, the crowd is mostly late baby boomers, who appre-

NIGHTLIFE ⟨ THE LOWDOWN

ciate not only the musical mix, but also the witty decor (ranging from the obvious—mounted sharks and neon beer signs—to a glass-enclosed patio adjacent the dance floor), as well as the changing mood from bar to bar (whose names aptly describe what to expect: Pool Shark Room, Shark Tank Room—with not one but three salt-water aquariums—and the Lava Room, with its seven-ties-style mirror balls and lava lamps). **Kiefer's Atop the Carriage House** appeals to anyone with a romantic streak, especially lithe, golf-tanned doctor and lawyer-types displaying their trophy wives and mistresses in the soft light.

For fortysomethings... **Gold Coast Dance Hall and Saloon** waltzes easily from country/western to big-band to ballroom evenings; even the decor has a touch of old-fashioned class, with wood-grained paneling and wrought-iron chandeliers. **French Quarter**, at the Four Queens Casino Hotel, is awash in N'Awlins ambience, especially when live jazz wafts through the charming patio on Mondays. The bar at **Play It Again, Sam** has become a discreet pickup spot for gentlemen with that distinguished touch of gray at the temples and ladies old enough to wear diamonds and get away with it. **Club Rio**'s strictly enforced dress code and wide range of music, from big band to lambada, makes this the premier place for the liposuction set to boogie the night away.

For lounge lizards... If you're looking for the Bill Murray-esque, lounge-merging-into-slump scene, try **The Continental Lounge** (a few blocks east of the Strip, between the Hilton and the hard Rock) for Cook E. Jarr and the Krums. Cook E. wears a black tuxedo without shirt or cummerbund, but with lots of gold necklaces and rings. With his knee-high, fire-engine-red boots, red hankie, and jet-black David Cassidy haircut, the self-pro-claimed "King of America's Lounges" mixes popular songs with somewhat off-color jokes and impressions and well-practiced banter for the mainly local, mainly middle-aged crowd. **Leroy's Satellite Sport's Lounge** is a tiny hole in the wall inside Howard Johnson's Hotel and Casino, with six small tables, a two-tray buffet with free food, and a large, blow-up beer can as a backdrop for the electric piano and vocalist. There's no dance floor, but the elderly locals don't seem to mind. The scene is livelier at **Koo Koos Lounge** at Vacation Village, on the Strip but way out of town. The small dance floor hops when Van Deguzman performs his one-man show on electric piano, sax, clarinet, and flute. The crowd is mostly local, but younger and more upbeat. It ain't slick, but that may be just the thing after a day at the MGM Grand.

Hot nightclubs... The city's three hottest nightclubs are all within an easy walk of the Strip's casino hotels, on the streets paralleling the east side of Las Vegas Boulevard. Since fitting a $300,000 roof over its cavernous courtyard area, **the Drink** has not only silenced its perpetually complaining neighbors in a condo complex across the street; it's also become the city's toughest place to get into, home of long, slow-moving lines. Inside, the Drink is a maze of seven separate bar environments, including a stand-up martini bar and cigar room. The music runs to local dance bands, peppered with a national touring group around once a week (disco nights fill up the empty spaces). If you're coming here on a weeknight, you should call ahead to see whether or not the Drink's open, as this place doesn't stay open all night, and will close early (for Vegas, that is), if the action's too slow. **The Beach** definitely lives up to its name. The moment you walk into this 24-hour nightclub/sports bar there's no mistaking that this is one place designed for pleasure—a slightly more mature version of spring break in Fort Lauderdale. Musically, live acts—both local and touring national bands—are booked into The Beach every week, though on most nights the driving music jumps around the dance spectrum, from the Cure to Stone Temple Pilots to Motown to INXS. The crowd here certainly knows how to gyrate, and do so with consummate abandon. If you're worrying about hitting 30, you're too old. The oldest surviving hotspot in Vegas's competitive nightclub scene is **The Shark**, a place whose racially mixed, impeccably dressed crowd of twenty- to fortysomethings parties to hip-hop/industrial/alternative sounds. The Shark's four bar areas are wrapped around a quiet outdoor patio, a multilevel urban dance club, a retro-Vegas lounge, and an intimate bar. The Shark developed a reputation as a "black" club, in no small part due to the overflow from the championship boxing matches taking place at the nearby MGM Grand or Caesars Palace, but

NIGHTLIFE ⟨ THE LOWDOWN

the club's entertainment mix attracts a diverse crowd, and everybody's welcome.

Moving up the charts... The hot newcomer on the Vegas nightclub scene is **Utopia**, a wild weekend club on the Strip that caters to the city's edgy, urban/gothic crowd. This is the sort of place that imports its DJs from L.A. and Chicago for one-night stands, drawing a 25-to-35 gay/straight/bi crowd dressed in black and heavy on the tattoos and Doc Martens. Utopia's lighting runs the gamut from tripped-out sixties psychedelia to the latest computerized gimmickery hooked up to the club's non-stop Euro-beat sound system—all overlaid with live drumming and guitar licks delivered by musicians sur-rounded by writhing dancers. It's far more enjoyable if you bring a date, since the attitude level can be either offensive or humorous, depending on the success of your pickup line. Keep an eye on the **Huntridge**, a concert and nightclub venue in a renovated downtown movie theater that's set to reopen its doors by 1997. Las Vegas, being the sort of city that falls head over heels for anything that's fresh and new, should hold true to form and swarm all over the Huntridge as soon as live acts start hitting its stage. Three years after it originally opened as a club in 1992, the Huntridge's roof collapsed (while the building was unoccupied), and the club's local owners have been making some heavyweight promises about the top-name acts they'll be bringing into town... which should make the folks at the Hard Rock's Joint quake in their Tony Lamas, and just may bring Vegas its first all-night venue for concerts and hanging out afterward.

Big is beautiful... Club **Rio** is the name given to the siz-zling scene that moves into the Rio's Copacabana Show-room (see Shows) from Wednesday through Sunday. Club Rio is Vegas's largest nightclub, with state-of-the art sound (a mix of urban disco, techno, and 1980s dance hits), video, and lights, as well as an atmosphere that suc-cessfully combines elements of a lounge with a nightclub and contemporary showroom. There's a dress code, so nobody wearing jeans and sneakers gets past the bouncer.

Painting the town pink... For the most part, Las Vegas's gay and lesbian clubs fit right into the "y'all come on down" category, with their mixed crowds (all ages, body types, ethnic compositions, and manners of dress, even a few stray straights), which is why the **Gipsy** stays so popular: It's friendly, unaffected, and comes across as just a great place to dance. The environment is urban/sophisticated, and the music covers the full range of popular dance hits, from 1980s trash disco to the very latest Euro-tunes imported (along with a few guys and gals) from L.A. and San Francisco. Expect to see more than a few of the Strip's male performers on Gipsy's dance floor—and not just those production-show dancers who twist and twirl with beautiful showgirls as a way to make a living, but also some of the biggest names on the Vegas Strip's entertainment scene (hint: grrrrr!). Gipsy has lots of special nights, making room for drag queens, lip-synchers, gay Latinos, and the beer-and-buns crew. Across the street from Gipsy you'll find the even more down-to-earth **Angles Lounge** (a k a Angles/Lace—Club Lace is the name of a lounge room and dance area attached to the back of Angles). Though the exterior says "basic neighborhood working-folks' hangout," this is actually Vegas's top lesbian nightclub, luring yet another melting pot to its several dance floors, patio, and pool tables. What Angles/Lace lacks in decor it more than makes up for in its unpretentious ambience and friendly clientele. And don't miss **Goodtimes**, if for no other reason than its rhinestone-studded location inside Liberace Plaza (where else?) and its kitschy disco nights on Fridays, Saturdays, and Mondays. The rest of the week, Goodtimes is your typical Vegas video-poker/neighborhood type place, but on disco nights, watch out!

Painting the town pink, in chaps and leather...

Here in the West, where many locals grew up around ranches and farms, country/western music is part of the culture, and that's why Vegas's gay cowboys and -girls two-step down to the **Texas Rodeo Saloon**, a club whose large dance floor turns out a ten-gallon-hat crowd for events like Underwear Night and Latino Fiesta Night. Vegas's up-and-coming gay nightspot is **Club Flex**, which lives up to its name with strippers, go-go dancers, and leather-clad bartenders. Daily drink specials and alternative music nights make it a popular choice with locals and tourists alike. And speaking of leather, Vegas's

NIGHTLIFE ✪ THE LOWDOWN

favorite leather-and-Levis bar is **The Buffalo**, an unassuming place within a minute's walk of the Gipsy. Definitely not a dance club and certainly not a women's bar, this joint is set up for gays who know what they like—and want to meet leather-minded individuals. Buffalo's also home to the Satyricons Motorcycle Club; along one wall are a few dozen snapshots of the Satyricons on their Harleys riding in Vegas's annual Toys for Tots parade (bikers with hearts!). A more mature gay crowd congregates at the **Backdoor**, a downtown, neighborhood video-poker bar that's also known as one of Vegas's best barbecue joints and has a more sedate music scene as well as an outdoor patio.

Blues in the night... The **Sand Dollar Lounge**, a Westside blues and bikers' bar, is the kind of place where men and women who like fast cars and loud motorcycles come to groove on blues musicians from across Vegas and the Southwest. Anyone would feel comfortable at the Sand Dollar (once they make it past the ornery bouncer and learn to avoid the eyes of the more belligerent drunks); the reward for finding this club is a very, very late night live music scene with cheap drinks, a cozy dance floor, and the genuine smoky ambiance of a tried-and-true blues joint. The city's largest blues bar (and the one that has the financial muscle to pull in the very best national touring acts from Chicago, New Orleans, New York, and San Francisco) is **Fremont Street Reggae & Blues**, a cavernous downtown nightclub that's divided on one side into a hybrid sports/reggae bar (three-pointer, mon), and on its other side into the best juke joint between Kansas City and Santa Monica. Acts like Junior Wells, the Paladins, William Clark, and Matt Murphy make regular stops here; on some nights it's possible to catch a great national blues act on one side of the Fremont Street, then slide over to the reggae side to dance a few ska numbers to a nationally known reggae band (but you'll have to pay two cover charges). On just about any night of the week this place has all the makings of great time: a varied, congenial crowd (from tourists to local arty types), great tunes, and a dark, sultry atmosphere.

All that jazz... Despite the glut of fine musicians (and occasional headliners like Wynton Marsalis stopping off at showrooms like the Aladdin) playing on and off the Strip, the city's most reliable jazz evening is Monday (which happens to be a convenient off night for many Vegas musicians). Start at the French Quarter room (or occasionally the Royal Pavillion Room) at the **Four Queens Casino Hotel**, a downtown venue that fronts on Fremont Street. The inventive promoter of Monday Night Jazz keeps juggling the evening's roster of musicians to allow both local and touring artists to jam together; what you usually get is top-quality jazz with some inspired riffs and several guest musicians jumping onstage for a number or two. Also on Monday nights, down Las Vegas Boulevard at the Riviera (which, in the face of the Disneyization of Vegas, now bills itself as "The Alternative for Grown-Ups"), Don Menza's Jazz on the Strip has become something of a local institution, playing the casino's **Le Bistro Lounge** from 9 till 1am, then making room for Lou Bronson's All-Star Band, a talented act that swings back and forth from R&B to jazz and oldies. MGM Grand's **Santa Fe Lounge** has one of the Strip's more imaginative Southwestern settings, in addition to a some fine local jazz combos. On the northwest side of town, the urbane, new-money crowd hanging out at the **North Beach Cafe** has developed a taste for jazz acts to match their hunger for merlot and duck confit. Local jazz combos (three-piece, usually) play three hours or so for the North Beach's cocktails crowd on Wednesday and Thursday nights; the latter is an open-mike showcase, when the vocals are likely to be handled by local yuppie attorneys longing for a chance to escape their dreary, litigation-filled lives for a more exciting existence in the spotlight. Even more out of the way is **Pogo's Tavern**, which has a Friday evening jazz scene featuring some of Vegas's older musicians jammin' with younger bloods in one of the smokiest environments this side of a Mickey Rourke film.

Sitting through stand-up... Not surprisingly, the top rungs of Vegas's comedy ladder are occupied by the showrooms hosting big-time acts: George Carlin, Dennis Miller, Rita Rudner, and Gilbert Gottfried are regulars, as are names that evoke the Vegas of days past, such as Don Rickles, Buddy Hackett, Rodney Dangerfield, and Bill Cosby. Two showrooms, Bally's **Celebrity Room** and the

NIGHTLIFE (THE LOWDOWN

Desert Inn's **Crystal Room**, are Vegas's best and most consistent bets for catching one of these stars, with the Tropicana's **Tiffany Theatre** and the Riviera's **Comedy Club** booking the same caliber of acts regularly, though not quite as consistently as the Desert Inn and Bally's. If you don't want to shell out $30 to see the live version of a comedian you've already caught a dozen times on HBO, check out one of the half dozen or so smaller clubs that have staked their reputations on showcasing comedy's lesser-known acts. These clubs are fun, sultry, and relaxed places to let loose a few howls at an affordable price; you may pay a small cover, but chances are that cover will include a drink or two (most clubs opt for the standard two-drink minimum). Maxim Casino Hotel's **Comedy Max** benefits from its easy parking situation, smaller dimensions, affable and pretty cocktail waitresses, and emphasis on young, in-your-face comedians. The shows at Max are for the earlybird crowd, but not so over at the Riviera's Comedy Club, where there's an anything-goes, let-it-all-hang-out, late-night attitude onstage and off. The Riv bills about half of its 11:45pm comedy-club acts as something called **XXXTREME Comedy**, where the humor revolves around masturbation, oral sex, and farting (and that's just for starters). The Riv's is also the most cutting-edge room in town, occasionally booking gay comics who draw strong crowds for these now-and-again late-night shows. On the less tasteless end of the comedy scale are the rooms at large hotel/casinos that book up-and-comers. MGM Grand's **Catch a Rising Star** is a very comfortable room that features acts you may have seen once or twice on some nationally syndicated television show, but whose faces are still much more familiar than are their names. (The Grand also offers great surreal experiences in its **Betty Boop Bar**: a Foster Brooks robot who delivers drinks along with a nonstop barrage of Catskills humor in 35-minute sets.) Harrah's **An Evening at the Improv** is affiliated with the same wildly successful comedy group in Chicago, and has for several years been a favorite with Vegas locals (who have avidly followed it from one Strip showroom to another). The Tropicana's **Comedy Stop at the Trop** is still considered a hotbed for the sort of comics who, in a year or two, will be packing them in over at the Strip's larger showrooms, yakking it up with Leno, or even starring in their very own sitcoms. Comedy Stop sets itself up as a competitive club, and shows featuring several comedians usually declare a winner for that night, keeping everyone from just going through the motions.

For the beery-eyed... While Vegas hasn't exactly embraced the microbrewery craze sweeping the nation (it requires you to sit in one place that's not a slot machine for far too long), there are a couple of local brewpubs that create their own ales and stouts. One, the **Holy Cow Brewery**, is located right on the Strip across the street from the Sahara. If you want a friendly atmosphere where locals and tourists mingle without getting in each others' way, as well as fantastic, heady brews that pour out of their taps ice cold, this cavernous place is great. The decor is bovine, everything proudly made in Jersey, as the staff quips. Another hangout for the microbrew crew is **Barley's**, a combined brewpub and full casino (only in Vegas) stuck in a suburban shopping mall in Green Valley, a 30-minute haul from the Strip. One of the Strip's newest hangouts, and a contender for Best Bar Atmosphere, is the **Monte Carlo Pub & Brewery**. It offers a brick-walled, urban warehouse look and about 20 taps pouring everything from the pub's own beers to an international selection of lagers, pilsners, ales, and such. The bar food is as good as it gets, there's a patio overlooking the casino's swimming pool (which is usually crowded with screaming kids), and a pair of dueling pianos for those who want to dance. The brewmeister spent several years working for outfits such as Samuel Adams. Two local pubs that don't brew their own beers, but which feature at least two dozen brews from around the world, as well as authentic pub atmospheres (and crowds), are the **Crown & Anchor British Pub** and the **Mad Dogs & Englishmen Pub**. Of the two, Crown & Anchor is the wee-hours champ, thanks to its all-night video-poker machines and Eastside location, a mere 10-minute drive off the Strip. The atmosphere here's pseudo-Tudor, with a clubby crowd that seems eager to socialize with anyone who walks through the doors. Mad Dogs is, as you can fathom from its name, a bit on the wilder side, despite similar Tudorish decor (beefeater statues, dart boards, heraldic banners) and a menu running toward fish and chips, bangers and mash, and roast beef and Yorkshire

NIGHTLIFE ⟨ THE LOWDOWN

pudding. This downtown bar lacks the gambling gear common in other Vegas pubs, which means it has to make its bread and butter the hard way—by selling beer. Unlike the more typical British-gentlemen's-club clientele at Crown & Anchor, the denizens of Mad Dogs lean more toward the streetwise—Brits and Aussies wearing tattoos and punk hair are frequent sightings, but they're blended in with some more normal looking regulars. There's another Mad Dogs & Englishmen Pub out on the west of town, for the suburban set.

From beans to boxing... The good old days of girl-versus-girl, baked-bean wrestling and other such sticky-floored decadence are essentially over in Las Vegas, replaced by "gentlemen's clubs" and exotic strip shows. Maybe it's part of the push to make Vegas more of a family destination, or maybe it's a sign of the increasing conservatism in this part of the country, or maybe the price of beans went up. Whatever the reason, the closest thing you'll find to mud wrestling now is Bikini Boxing Night at **The Beach**, which is a pretty raucous place to be sure, but hardly a low-rent joint. The crowd is mixed local and tourist, and the boxing is pretty tame.

Fleshpits for guys... The rest of the legal sex-show action takes place in Vegas's strip clubs, though most adopt a hands-off policy—once customers have purchased several snifters full of Grand Marnier for their temporary companion (and if it's an all-nude club, that'll be Snapple rather than Grand Marnier). One partial exception is the somewhat notorious **Palomino Club** on the north end of Las Vegas Boulevard. Due to a grandfather clause, this is the only *all*-nude club which allows you to drink anything harder than Snapple. Because the venerable club's located just outside the city limits, the Palomino is also governed by another Clark County strip-joint rule, which allows patrons to touch certain of the dancers' body parts (legs and arms, depending on what the dancer permits). Cultural anthropologists who drop for a little research at the Palomino on a weekend around 2am will be able to document touch-me lap-dance action happening all over the club. Inside the city limits, the action's much tamer, although the dancers (all dreaming, no doubt, of their big break in *Jubilee!* or *Folies Bergère*) are usually more attractive than their counterparts elsewhere in the country. The most popular club in town—attracting the youngest, rowdiest crowd—is **Cheetah's Topless Lounge**. Many of the dancers here have worked in the Strip's better showrooms, but this is where they perform all the wicked moves they can't get away with elsewhere. The dancers at the **Crazy Horse Saloon** are a mixed group of pros working the West's topless circuit and some hardened local dancers who have been stuck here way too long, lending it a rather impersonal, humorless air. In contrast, **Olympic Garden Cabaret**, located right on the Strip, is loaded with personable dancers working a sophisticated room that features a half-dozen dance platforms. This place starts going in late afternoon; it's a favored hangout of the I-just-got-off-work-and-need-a-drink crowd from the courthouse just up the street. Finally, there's **Club Paradise**, which bills itself as a "gentlemen's club" and even ropes off a VIP section (with a minimum of $50 per person in drinks). How classy is this joint? Well, seating is by maitre d', there are actual armchairs—with genuine upholstery—rather than stools, jazz groups play between dance acts, and the murals of couples (and threesomes) *in flagrante delicto* are termed "erotic art." And, oh yes, there are more than 100 dancers over the course of the evening. No wonder it's conventioneer city.

Fleshpits for gals... Not a town to discriminate in going after your pay-for-prurience dollar, there are also places for women to watch buff dancers take it off. Those princes of booty shakin', the Chippendales Dancers, have set up a regular Vegas-style production show at **The Beach**. Taking place daily (except Thursdays) from 6 to 9pm, this is the type of entertainment that is called a "full show" here; that means specially designed lighting, sound and costumes for the ten Chippendales studs... sort of like a beefcake version of *Jubilee!* (see The Show Scene). The only drawback is the $25 ticket price, which doesn't even include a free drink. Meanwhile, the **Olympic Garden Cabaret** has a room with male strippers, adjacent to where its female dancers work (see above). It's an intimate space with a small stage, tables, and a personable atmosphere that is complemented by the seemingly jolly attitude brought by the largely female audience of locals and tourists.

NIGHTLIFE ⟨ THE LOWDOWN

The tourist's strip... Below the supposed class of the "gentlemen's clubs," there's another level of strip joint that caters mainly to tourists—tourists who don't know any better. **Deja Vu Showgirls** is an all-nude club with Wet T-Shirt nights on Thursdays and shower dances all the time. **The Can-Can Room** is another all-nude club, with one runway and lots of ladies hard-selling patrons for private dances. No matter how persuasively the dancers claim customers'll be getting up close and personal, they won't be. **Club Exotica** advertises itself as "A New Generation of Social Encounter." They also tout "The Body Sex Show" every Thursday night. This all-nude club, which has, on occasion, a Penthouse Pet or Miss Universe dancing, neither has a sex show, nor is it a new generation of anything. And remember, all of the above all-nude establishments are not allowed to serve alcohol.

The local's strip... Two low-pressure places which feature nudity are **The Tender Trap**, a small topless club, and **The Tally-Ho**, an all-nude dancing establishment (again, no alcohol here). The Tender Trap has one stage surrounded by the bar and a few comfy chairs in the corners. Following their routines, the girls come over to the bar and ask each patron if they want a private dance. They're polite and friendly and not out to harass you. The Tally-Ho is equally small and low key, with seven to a dozen girls at a time dancing under the poor lighting.

Sports bars with action... Every casino has what's known as its "sportsbook" area, which is usually set up as a bizarre collection of library desks, video screens, electronic tote boards, cashiers' desks, and a bar against the back wall. If you want to see the prototype for many of the nation's modern sports bars, step into the **Las Vegas Hilton**'s or the **MGM Grand**'s sportsbook. But, take note, sportsbooks are no-nonsense places where gamblers have thousands of bucks riding on a day's action—they're hardly the sort of joints you go to for some loud-mouthed relaxation with friends and teammates. For that kind of action, residents' two favorite places are **LJ's Sports Bar & Grill** on the Westside and the **Final Score Sports Bar** inside Sam's Town Casino Hotel on the Eastside. The Final Score is the hands-down winner, with wood floors, a regulation-size basketball court for two players, a sand-volleyball pit (gee, who needs a gym?), pool tables, air hockey, electronic darts, lots of funky sports memorabilia, and live entertainment on weekends. LJ's has better pub grub, but that, the autographed 8-by-10s all over the place, and the dozens of TV monitors can't compensate for the sterile atmosphere.

Best for one-night bands... No question: It's **The Joint** at the Hard Rock. The acts at the opening alone included The Eagles, Melissa Etheridge, B.B. King, Iggy Pop, and Sheryl Crow. Standards have hardly declined since, with the likes of Bob Dylan, Ziggy Marley, Hootie and the Blowfish, and James Brown bringing down the house. **The Railhead** is where locals head to escape *las turistas;* the musical menu at this cherished secret is as varied as it gets at smaller venues, including Morris Day, Night Ranger, and Charlie Daniels. Swagger through the doors of the **Frisco Saloon** and you'll swear time somehow froze a couple of decades back, but it's actually *the* most jumpin' hangout for the heavy-metal/slamdance crowd. Surprisingly good young bands do Led Zep covers as well as their own material on the tiny stage. Occasionally, a hard-edged thrash scene moves into **Mad Dogs & Englishmen**, where the city's alternative scene gravitates whenever the right band's playing. On the Eastside, **Tiger's Pub** roars with up-and-coming alternative bands (some L.A. and Phoenix groups mixed in with local newcomers). Right on the Strip, the **Turf Lounge VIP Room**, inside the Jockey Club, is home to the city's gothic/vampire scene... mostly made up of UNLV students and some truly dangerous loser types. Don't worry about someone taking a swing at you, though—the Jockey Club's security keeps a lid on things.

NIGHTLIFE (THE LOWDOWN

The Index

Aladdin Lounge. This live-music hangout on the Strip attracts a great crowd on nights when rock acts play the casino's theater. Other nights, you're better off heading elsewhere.... *Tel 702/736–0111. Aladdin, 3667 Las Vegas Blvd. S. Open until 4am.*

Angles Lounge. Predominately a lesbian bar, Angles keeps a mixed crowd out in front among pool tables and video games, and a women's club in the back.... *Tel 702/791–0100. 4633 Paradise Rd. Open 24 hours.*

Baccarat Bar. A sophisticated lounge set amidst the Mirage's South Pacific-themed rain forest interior. A good place to meet people who might be needing people very late at night.... *Tel 702/791–7111. 3400 Las Vegas Blvd. S.. Open until 4am.*

Backdoor. This neighborhood gay bar has a mixed crowd of young and older men and women. A sociable place serving some of the best barbecue in Vegas.... *Tel 702/385–2018. 1415 E. Charleston Blvd. Open 24 hours.*

Barley's. Worth a visit to Green Valley (about 30 minutes from the Strip) just to see how a very modern, only-in-Vegas concept of wedging a brewpub right smack into the middle of a casino can work.... *Tel 702/458–2739. 4500 E. Sunset Rd. Open 24 hours.*

The Beach. If you can handle the rowdy atmosphere of a college-town nightclub, you're going to love this place. Waitresses wear bikinis, male bartenders go shirtless, dance music pounds relentlessly, and the beer never stops flowing.... *Tel 702/731–1925. 365 Convention Center Dr. Open 24 hours.*

Betty Boop Bar. Another of MGM Grand's tricky concepts, Ms. Betty's place features a robot whose imitation of the highly sauced Foster Brooks keeps all the tourists in stitches—for a while, at least.... *Tel 702/891–1111. MGM Grand, 3799 Las Vegas Blvd. S. Open until 4am.*

Big Sky Lounge. Country/western live-music club with line dancing, western outfits, and big hair galore.... *Tel 702/ 380–7777. Stratosphere, 2000 Las Vegas Blvd. S. Open until 3am.*

The Buffalo. Exclusively male leather-and-Levis bar; home to the Satyricons, a bikers' club.... *Tel 702/733–8355. 4640 Paradise Rd. Open 24 hours.*

The Can-Can Room. A hard-sell, all-nude joint, where the dancers push hard for private dances that run from $50 for about 10 minutes to $100 for half an hour, and $150 for an hour. You might learn the Macarena, but that's about all you'll get. The cover is $10, which includes one soft drink.... *Tel 702/737–1161. 155 Industrial Rd. Open until 5am.*

Captain Morgan's. This kitsch-filled place inside Treasure Island has the sort of "Pirates of Penzance-gone-Vegas" decor that will shiver your timbers and make you wonder if you'll ever get back to Kansas.... *Tel 702/894–7111; 3300 Las Vegas Blvd. S.. Open until 4am.*

Catch a Rising Star. As you'd expect, this comedy club is part of the national chain that gives young comedians a chance to hone their acts until that day when Jay Leno's producer rings.... *Tel 702/891–1111. MGM Grand, 3799 Las Vegas Blvd. S.*

Celebrity Room. Everything at Bally's is done right, and its Celebrity Room becomes one of the city's top comedy clubs when it books acts like George Carlin and Penn and Teller.... *Tel 702/739–4111. Bally's, 2645 Las Vegas Blvd. S.*

Cheetah's Topless Lounge. The city's most popular topless club attracts a young, mostly workingmen's crowd for its rock-and-roll atmosphere.... *Tel 702/384–0074. 2112 Western Ave. Open 24 hours.*

Chippendales at The Beach. A legendary company of male dancers doing their full production show, complete with those left over Village People costumes, special lighting and sound effects.... *Tel 702/731–1925. 365 Convention Center Drive. Nightly (except Thur) from 6 to 9pm. $25 cover.*

Cleopatra's Barge. For years, this live-music lounge inside Caesars Palace has been a local favorite, not only for its floating dance floor but also because of the reliable pickup scene that's here nearly every night until 4am.... *Tel 702/731–7110. Caesars Palace, 3570 Las Vegas Blvd. S.*

Club Exotica. The occasional *Penthouse* Pet who drops by to dance doesn't make up for the very average stage, dancers, and ambience at this all-nude club. There's a $10 cover and $10 minimum. Semi-private dances cost $10 and a couch dance costs $20.... *Tel 702/252–8559. 3100 Sirius Rd. Open until 4am weekdays, 6am Fridays and Saturdays.*

Club Flex. The nonstop action at this club isn't particularly friendly to straights (unlike Gipsy), but lesbians and gay males flock here for cheap drinks, great DJs, and special nights seven times weekly.... *Tel 702/385–3539. 4371 W. Charleston Blvd. Open until 5am.*

Club Paradise. High cover charges, high drink prices, and a high quotient of horny businessmen in town for that big convention are this joint's calling cards.... *Tel 702/734–7990. 4416 Paradise Rd. Open 24 hours.*

Club Rio. On certain nights (especially Wednesday), this is where Vegas's hottest scene takes place. A huge place with state-of-the-art video and sound, Club Rio also has a dress code, thankfully.... *Tel 702/252–7777. Rio Suites, 3700 W. Flamingo Rd. Open until 5am.*

Comedy Club. This comedy room inside the Riviera is the closest thing you'll find in Vegas to the smoke-filled yuk-yuk rooms of years past. Books an occasional headliner act like Gilbert Gottfried or Bobcat Goldthwait.... *Tel 702/734–5110. Riviera, 2901 Las Vegas Blvd. S.*

Comedy Max. Located just a couple of blocks off the Strip, Comedy Max is well worth searching for because it's one of the nation's top proving grounds for young, on-the-way-up comedians.... *Tel 702/731–4300. Maxim, 160 E. Flamingo Rd.*

Comedy Stop at the Trop. This Strip comedy club is part of a national chain specializing in young talent, so you're taking your chances when buying a ticket.... *Tel 702/739–2222. Tropicana, 3801 Las Vegas Blvd. S.*

The Continental Lounge. Cook E. Jarr and the Krums headline here, which should tell you something. A fascinating stop on any tour of the lower lights of the town.... *Tel 702/737–5555. 4100 Paradise Rd. Open until 2:30am.*

Crazy Horse Saloon. The closest topless club to the Strip, Crazy Horse attracts lots of Japanese businessmen and conventioneers.... *Tel 702/732–1116. 4034 Paradise Rd. Open 24 hours.*

Crown & Anchor British Pub. A very friendly neighborhood bar serving nearly three dozen fresh drafts from around the world, plus great food.... *Tel 702/739–8676. 1350 E. Tropicana Ave. Open 24 hours.*

Crystal Room. After former owner Howard Hughes died, the Desert Inn became part of the Sheraton hotel chain, and it's successfully staked its claim to a share of the Strip's headliner comedy action. Dennis Miller is a regular, as is Rita Rudner.... *Tel 702/733–4444. Desert Inn, 3145 Las Vegas Blvd. S.*

Cyber City Cafe. A coolsters' hangout close to the UNLV campus. A great place to check your e-mail or meet a geeky date.... *Tel 702/732–2001. 3945 S. Maryland Pkwy. Open 24 hours.*

Deja Vu Showgirls. Touristy all-nude club with wet T-shirt nights and shower dances. A $10 entry fee and a $10 beverage charge lets you have a bottomless glass of soda pop all night long. Extra dances start at $15.... *Tel 702/894–4167. 3247 S. Industrial Rd. Open until 4am.*

Don Menza's Jazz on the Strip. See **Le Bistro Lounge.**

Drink & Eat Too. Despite its goofy name (locals just say "the Drink"), this enormous nightclub attracts nearly everyone.

THE INDEX

NIGHTLIFE

Some nights it's the city's best-dressed crowd, while on others it's T-shirt time. Worth checking out, especially for its cigar bar.... *Tel 702/796–5519. 200 E. Harmon Ave. Open until 5am.*

Dylan's Dance Hall & Saloon. This country/western nightclub on the Boulder Strip attracts a serious line-dancing crowd, and is a logical place to wind up if you tire of the action at the larger, nearby western dance clubs at Boulder Station and Sam's Town.... *Tel 702/451–4006. 4660 Boulder Hwy. Open 24 hours.*

An Evening at the Improv. This Vegas outpost of the Chicago-based improv group specializes in young talent, audience participation, and inoffensive humor.... *Tel 702/369–5000. Harrah's, 3475 Las Vegas Blvd. S.*

Final Score Sports Bar. A very cool sports bar with all the bells and whistles imaginable—video games, pool tables, basketball hoop, great burgers, and lots of different draft beers.... *Tel 702/456–7777. Sam's Town, 5111 Boulder Hwy. Open until 2am or later.*

Fremont Street Reggae & Blues. Las Vegas's numero-uno live-music club for a wide range of local, regional, and national acts covering not only blues and reggae, but also R&B and some rock music as well. Check it out for first-rate performances by top recording artists.... *Tel 702/594–4640. 400 E. Fremont St. Open until 4am.*

French Quarter. A Glitter Gulch casino hotel, and on Monday nights, this city's leading jazz outpost, with a steady four- or five-piece combo being joined by guest musicians for three sets.... *Tel 702/385–4011. Four Queens, 202 E. Fremont St. Open until 2am.*

Frisco Saloon. The city's most popular nightclub for the heavy-metal crowd and local garage bands—come here to see wild-haired men and women in their 20s and 30s rockin' out to Zep.... *Tel 702/382–6962. 332 W. Sahara Ave. Open 24 hours.*

Gipsy. The city's premier gay nightclub, Gipsy has a mixed crowd and lots of friendly bartenders working a neon-lit, urbanesque club that turns on its afterburners around 1am, blasting away till dawn.... *Tel 702/731–1919. 4605 Paradise Rd. S. Open 24 hours.*

Gold Coast Dance Hall & Saloon. Right off the Strip, this geezers' paradise is inside the Gold Coast casino hotel, one of Vegas's best bets for cheap, good food and down-home attitudes. It does have a huge dance floor, though. If you get bored here, you can wander down to another part of the hotel and go bowling.... *Tel 702/367–7111. Gold Coast, 4000 W. Flamingo Rd. Open until 3am.*

Goodtimes. Fulfill all your Liberace fantasies at Goodtimes, located in the same Flamingo Road shopping center where the glittery one established his museum and favorite restaurant serving mama's recipes.... *Tel 702/736–9494. 1775 E. Tropicana Ave. Open until 4am.*

Holy Cow Brewery. This combination brewpub/hamburger joint on the Strip serves the coldest fresh-brewed beer in Vegas, attracting a loyal crowd of friendly locals.... *Tel 702/732–2697. 2423 Las Vegas Blvd. S. Open 24 hours.*

Horse A-Round Bar. This tourist-filled watering hole inside Circus Circus is one of the few places on the grounds of this mega–casino hotel where Mom and Dad can get a moment's relief from the perpetual kid-oriented madness reigning outside.... *Tel 702/734–0410. Circus Circus, 2880 Las Vegas Blvd. S. Open until 3am.*

Huntridge. Once the favored hangout for Vegas's hip set, the Huntridge will become a live-music club to again rival the Hard Rock when it finishes replacing its fallen-in roof.... *Tel 702/477–7703. 1208 E. Charleston Blvd.*

Images Cabaret. Tucked off the Strat's casino floor, Images is home to celebrity impersonators early in the evening, then switches gears into a live-music club from around midnight to 4am.... *Tel 702/380–7777. Stratosphere, 2000 Las Vegas Blvd. S.*

Ipanema Bar. Classy joint inside the Rio, loaded with the expected decor that charges your Ricky Ricardo-meets-Ida

Lupino fantasies.... *Tel 702/252–7777. 3700 W. Flamingo Rd.. Open until 4am.*

Jimmy Murphy's Bar. This alternative nightclub is the sort of place where the bouncers frisk everyone, and check everyone's ID. Heavy on local bands.... *Tel 702/258–6344. 6138 W. Charleston Blvd. Open until 3am.*

The Joint. Attracting the city's hippest crowd for live-music shows, The Joint is where Vegas's chic set parties early in the evening, before heading out to one of the city's many all-night clubs.... *Tel 702/693–5000. Hard Rock Hotel, 4455 Paradise Rd.*

Kiefer's Atop the Carriage House. This solid standby of the local fine-dining scene will remind you of the kinds of places your folks brought you to when you were just a snotty-nosed kid. Lots of flaming desserts, but also a quiet piano bar with a great view of the lower Strip, and a nice retreat from Vegas's prevailing nuttiness.... *Tel 702/739–8000. 105 E. Harmon Ave. Open until 3am.*

Koo Koos Lounge. Van Deguzman's one-man show on electric piano, sax, clarinet, and flute keeps young, un-hip but happy locals on the small dance floor.... *Tel 702/897–1700. Vacation Village, 6711 S. Las Vegas Blvd. Open 24 hours.*

Lagoon Saloon. The Mirage's watering hole, smack in the middle of a Vegas-style, faux rain forest. You've got to see it to believe it.... *Tel 702/791–7111. 3400 Las Vegas Blvd. S.. Open until 4am.*

La Piazza Lounge. A piano bar at night, and home to local jazz great Ghalib Ghallab during the early evening, La Piazza is the most secluded spot inside Caesars Palace, making it a favorite meeting place for all sorts of local professionals.... *Tel 702/731–7110. Caesars Palace, 3570 Las Vegas Blvd. S. Open until 4am.*

Las Vegas Hilton Sportsbook. This huge gambling hall is a comfortable, action-filled place to watch the big games on Saturday and Sunday on a dozen enormous video screens.... *Tel 702/732–5111. Las Vegas Hilton, 3000 Paradise Rd. Open 24 hours.*

NIGHTLIFE / THE INDEX

Leroy's Satellite Sport's Lounge. If you're looking for somewhere low-key to hide from the tourists, this could be the place. In the Howard Johnson's hotel, the lounge is small, local, and slow.... *Tel 702/798–1111. 3111 W. Tropicana Blvd. Open until midnight on weekends.*

Le Bistro Lounge. Setting up shop on Monday nights in the Riviera's Le Bistro Lounge, Don Menza and his regular jazz combo draw big-name guest artists who are playing elsewhere on the Strip. Lou Bronsons All-Star Band swings into action at 1am on Monday and Saturday nights.... *Tel 702/734–5110. Riviera, 2901 Las Vegas Blvd. S. Open until 4am.*

L'Isles Bar. Unlike the rest of the Stratosphere, L'Isles, with its Caribbean-music backdrop, is one place where the atmosphere can deceive you into thinking you're a half-continent removed from the Strip.... *Tel 702/380–7777. Stratosphere, 2000 Las Vegas Blvd. S. Open until 4am.*

LJ's Sports Bar & Grill. One of the city's most popular sports bars is a disappointing place, with lots of TV sets and some half-hearted memorabilia displays.... *Tel 702/871–1424. 4405 W. Flamingo Rd. Open 24 hours.*

Mad Dogs & Englishmen Pub. Rowdy, young-person's beer palace with a lively music scene on weekends, as well as lots of Aussies, Brits, and other specimens from the Queen's domain.... *Tel 702/382–5075. 515 Las Vegas Blvd. S. Open until 3am.*

Mambo's Lounge. If you need a break from Club Rio's sleek setting, Club Mambo is another of the Rio's lounges, but with a more subdued atmosphere.... *Tel 702/252–7777. Rio Suites, 3700 W. Flamingo Rd. Open until 4am.*

MGM Grand sportsbook. Bright and cheerful, MGM's sportsbook has a wholesome, family feel, as well as very comfortable seats.... *Tel 702/891–1111. MGM Grand, 3799 Las Vegas Blvd. S. Open 24 hours.*

Minstrel's Lounge. Some things the Excalibur does right, some not so right. Minstrel's Lounge works because this megaresort pumps big bucks into booking strong dance bands, and

NIGHTLIFE ⎰ THE INDEX

keeps them playing until 4am.... *Tel 702/597–7777. Excalibur, 3850 Las Vegas Blvd. S.*

Monte Carlo Pub & Brewery. One of the best places to hang out on the Strip, this brewpub inside the new Monte Carlo casino has an industrial warehouse feel that's a perfect setting for its great homebrews and wood-fired pizzas.... *Tel 702/730–7777. Monte Carlo, 3770 Las Vegas Blvd. S. Open until 3am.*

Nefertiti's Lounge. The Luxor's pharaoh-on-vacation theme gets a little tiresome at times, but that shouldn't stop you from hitting this fairly lively lounge inside the world's largest pyramid.... *Tel 702/262–4000. 3900 Las Vegas Blvd. S.. Open until 4am.*

The Nightclub. One of the best casino lounges for live music acts, The Nightclub attracts a mixed crowd of locals and tourists staying upstairs inside the Las Vegas Hilton.... *Tel 702/732–5111. Las Vegas Hilton, 3000 Paradise Rd.. Open until 4am on weekends.*

North Beach Cafe. One of the favored hangouts for the city's yuppie lawyer/real-estate developer/marketing-executive crowd, the North Beach Cafe is also home to Wednesday and Thursday jazz-combo nights, usually with one of those nights dedicated to new local talent.... *Tel 702/247–9530. 2605 S. Decatur Blvd. Open until 1am.*

Olympic Garden Cabaret. This club at least offers something for everyone: nasty girls on one side, nasty boys on the other. Famous as a deal-making meeting ground for the city's movers and shakers.... *Tel 702/385–8987. 1531 Las Vegas Blvd. S. Open 24 hours.*

Palomino Club. Topless, bottomless... and they serve alcohol here—thanks to a grandfather clause, the only all-nude club in town allowed to pour booze.... *Tel 702/642–2984. 1848 Las Vegas Blvd. N. Open 24 hours.*

Peppermill Inn's Fireside Lounge. This longtime favorite resting-up spot for the Strip's working folks is a fifties-style step back in time... to the days of wine, roses, and guys named Vinny in ill-fitting suits.... *Tel 702/735–4177. 2985 Las Vegas Blvd. S. Open 24 hours.*

Pisces Bistro. Locals avoid this place, but if you want to bump into the Japanese salaryman of your dreams living it up on his expense account and hanging out in a lounge that, from time to time, attracts Hollywood types in town for a shoot, this is your kinda place.... *Tel 702/796–3300. 375 E. Harmon Ave. Open 24 hours.*

Play it Again, Sam. This neighborhood piano bar has kept more than a few local musicians busy during their "between gigs" months away from the Strip. You may have to sing along with the crowd, but that's half the fun.... *Tel 702/876–1550. 4120 Spring Mountain Rd. Open 24 hours.*

Pogo's Tavern. This smoke-filled joint will meet anyone's expectations of a what a seedy, neighborhood jazz club should look (and smell) like. Of course, it delivers where it counts: great jams and a knowledgeable crowd.... *Tel 702/646–9735. 2103 N. Decatur Blvd. Jazz performed only on weekends, when open into the early morning hours.*

The Railhead. Sounds like a leather bar or even a country/western joint, but Railhead is actually one of the few Vegas lounges regularly booking African-American R&B acts, mixing these pros with their rock and country/western brethren.... *Tel 702/432–7777. Boulder Station, 4111 Boulder Hwy. Open 24 hours.*

Rockabilly's. Another of the Boulder Strip's cowboy bars, Rockabilly's is considered the most commercialized of them all, with a musical focus on country/western pop acts like Billy Ray Cyrus and all those other achey-breaky big-haired studs.... *Tel 702/641–5800. 3785 Boulder Hwy. Open 24 hours.*

Sam's Town Western Dance Hall. One of Vegas's most popular country/western music clubs, the crowd here tends toward serious dancers... the type who enter (and place in) national dance competitions.... *Tel 702/456–7777. 5111 Boulder Highway. Open until 4am.*

Sand Dollar Lounge. This great blues bar attracts a tough-looking but respectful crowd that loves great music and likes listening to bands until dawn.... *Tel 702/871–6651. 3355 Spring Mountain Rd. Open 24 hours.*

Santa Fe Lounge. An open-sided lounge that makes a grab for a Southwestern feeling. On a pedestrian walkway, this place is hardly the kind of setting for quiet romance, but it does book good bands.... *Tel 702/891–1111. MGM Grand, 3799 Las Vegas Blvd. S. Open until 3am.*

Shark. This is one of the few places in Las Vegas's nightclub scene where you'll want to look your best. Shark has an urban, multiethnic clientele ranging from late 20s to late 40s that switches its musical tastes from hip hop to alternative to straight rock.... *Tel 702/795–7525. 75 E. Harmon Ave. Open until 3am.*

Starlight Lounge. Want to get a glimpse of Vegas's past and middle-class future, all rolled up into one place? Then hit the Stardust's Starlight Lounge, where local ranchers crowd up against holidaying, overweight egg salesmen from Iowa, boogeying away until the Vegas dawn.... *Tel 702/732-6111. 3000 Las Vegas Blvd. S. Open until 4am.*

The Tally-Ho. A small, locals-oriented topless dancing joint. Admission is $10, with a one-drink minimum. Dances in the private rooms run from $65 for a half hour and up, plus tip.... *Tel 702/792–9330. 2580 S. Highland Dr.. Open 24 hours.*

The Tender Trap. Another small, topless dancing place frequented mostly by locals. They have one stage, a bar, and some comfy chairs. No cover and no minimum.... *Tel 702/ 732–1111. 311 E. Flamingo Rd. Open 24 hours.*

Texas Rodeo Saloon. Gay country/western nightclubs are one of the more interesting aspects of nightlife culture in the West. This club lives up to all the usual Vegas expectations, with a *muy*-macho atmosphere and lotsa beer.... *Tel 702/ 456–5525. 3430 E. Tropicana Ave. Open 24 hours.*

Tiffany Theatre. An on-again-off-again venue for top names in the comedy world. When they're in town, Don Rickles and Buddy Hackett perform here.... *Tel 702/739–2222. Tropicana, 3801 Las Vegas Blvd. S.*

Tiger's Pub. Favored hangout of the UNLV alternative-music crowd, featuring live bands on weekends.... *Tel 702/438–0355. 4885 E. Lake Mead Blvd. Open until 3am.*

NIGHTLIFE ⌣ THE INDEX

Tropics Lounge. The sort of place where you half expect Jimmy Buffet to pop out of the woodwork, this live-music club fits right in with the Trop's slightly askew, but eminently enjoyable, atmosphere.... *Tel 702/739–2222. Tropicana, 3801 Las Vegas Blvd. S. Open until 4am.*

Turf Lounge VIP Room. This Strip nightclub is Vegas's top venue for touring heavy-metal and grunge acts blowing in from L.A. for one-night stands.... *Tel 702/736–3899. 3700 Las Vegas Blvd. S. Open 24 hours.*

Tut's Hut. This small Polynesian-themed bar (no, you're not hallucinating) inside the Luxor's "World's Largest Pyramid" is hardly worth going out of your way for, unless you're already inside the big glass tomb. If you do stop by, you're guaranteed to see pink (the color of the neon trim).... *Tel 702/ 262–4000; 3800 Las Vegas Blvd. S. Open until 3am.*

Utopia. Here's where you can have your nipples pierced while waiting for a tattooed bartender to pour you a neon martini, then dance with the gothic crew until dawn.... *Tel 702/593– 5835. 3765 Las Vegas Blvd. S. Open until 6am.*

XXXTREME Comedy. Pssst... wanna hear jokes about sexual positions, barfing, other bodily functions, and death?... *Tel 702/734–5110. Riviera, 2901 Las Vegas Blvd. S. Call for showtimes.*

NIGHTLIFE ⟋ THE INDEX

the

arts

4

Here's a multiple choice
question: What's the Las
Vegas definition of
the arts? a) Liberace's
candelabra collection;
b) The special effects of
eponymous Broadway

clone *EFX*, starring ex-Phantom Michael Crawford; c) The gold chains on Wayne Newton's bodyguards; d) All of the above; e) None of the above. If you answered d *and* e, you hit the jackpot. If your mental image of Las Vegas is of a seamless tapestry of neon-lit glitz and glamour, you'll be surprised to find that beneath this city's highly promoted exterior do lurk the seeds of a cultural core. Certainly, the Vegas of days past was a place where hardly anybody cared or thought much about such cultural pursuits as contemporary dance, theater, and fine arts. But the yearly arrival of nearly 100,000 new residents has meant that Vegas now has a reason (translation: financial and audience support) to begin searching for artistic expressions that are oriented to entertain those who live here, not just those who visit. The preeminent art form here is, without question, dance. Vegas is a place where lots of dancers, theater technicians, gaffers, costumers, directors, and acoustic designers can now make a living from the many production shows, as well as from the special events staged throughout the city. It's largely these pros who have also spun off a local arts scene, some of which takes place in the city's neighborhood arts centers, and other parts of which are staged outdoors during the warmer months at one of the several very popular outdoor performance facilities scattered about Las Vegas. Traditional arts such as orchestral and chamber music are harder to find, as is serious theater; local and community productions tend to be the standard. If you have to see a *pas de deux* or hear something unsynthesized, this city is now big enough to accommodate you. But if your standards are offended by anything less than world or national class music or dance...well, hit those tables harder so as to be able to buy ticket subscriptions to the ballet or opera back home in Chicago, New York, or San Francisco. In the meantime, be satisfied with the Wagnerian scale of the big production shows.

Getting Tickets

With the exception of mega-concert acts such as the Stones, Red Hot Chili Peppers, and Alanis, we're not exactly talking about a mad rush. If Mick and the boys ever get back to the MGM Grand, acting early and fast to line up your seats is going to be mandatory. But for the most part, performing-arts events in Las Vegas are not going to require you to grease someone's palm or camp overnight in front of a ticket booth. Simply call or stroll up to the box office for your performance of choice. Even if there aren't great seats available for the show you're wanting to see on the day of performance, check the cancellations at the will-call window. Get there an hour before curtain and those released tickets should be yours.

Sources

The daily newspaper most everyone around here reads is the *Review-Journal,* which is the morning counterpart to the afternoon newspaper, *The Sun* (which hardly anybody reads). The *R-J,* as locals call it, devotes a good chunk of its business reportage to Vegas casinos and hotels, and whenever someone hits a big jackpot on a slot machine, the *R-J* manages to cover that as well. For nightcrawlers, the *R-J*'s "Weekend" section, published on Fridays as an insert, is an absolute must. Besides the most comprehensive, up-to-date calendar of what's taking place in the city's lounges, showrooms, nightclubs, discos, concert halls, outdoors performance stages, art centers, and coffeehouses, "Weekend" also offers the fantastic local arts coverage of Mike Paskevich and Mike Weatherford, entertainment reporters whose individual abilities to make-or-break a Vegas band, production show, nightclub or restaurant are the stuff of local legend. Check the *R-J* throughout the week for arts and entertainment updates and changes of scheduled showtimes and acts.

The city's best freebie publications for anyone wanting to tune into the local music and arts scene are the weekly *New Times* and the monthly *Scope,* easily found all around Las Vegas, especially at bars, coffeeshops, and record stores. *New Times* is known for its strong coverage of the city's live theater and classical music scenes, as well as for its movie and restaurant reviews. And, as you'd find in any weekly worth its salt, *New Times* also devotes a large chunk of editorial space to insightful coverage of the Las Vegas political, environmental, social and media scenes.

Scope has a decidedly more urban edge to its coverage of the city's arts and entertainment scenes, treating everything from gay bars to thrash bands and lounge acts with the same equanimity. A monthly publication, *Scope*'s entertainment calendar is comprehensive when it comes to exhibitions and performances in the city's art galleries, theaters, and libraries.

THE ARTS ⟩ INTRODUCTION

The Lowdown

Where it's at... The big bopper is the **Thomas & Mack Center**, the Madison Square Garden wannabe that also hosts the UNLV Running Rebels hoopsters (see Sports). This is the main venue for touring rock bands mounting large-scale shows, from AC/DC to ZZ Top; production values and acoustics are generally excellent. Thomas & Mack (see Sports) is a multipurpose arena, so whenever pro wrestling comes to town, whenever the Las Vegas Thunder hockey team has a home game, or whenever local heartthrob Andre Agassi (voted the No. 1 Las Vegas male that Las Vegas women would most want to spend a night with) is playing in a tournament here, Thomas & Mack is the place of choice. Don't expect anything much in the way of amenities—that's a matter better addressed by the casino/hotel venues down on the Strip. But if you're one of 18,776 screaming, beer-slopping rock fans who need a place to party, this is the only place in town that will accommodate you. **The Joint at the Hard Rock Casino Hotel** is the busiest of the Strip's more "intimate" concert halls, accommodating up to 1,400 people for acts ranging from Bob Dylan to Ted Nugent, in a setting that's not only spacious, but also perfectly designed as a multipurpose nightclub and live-music venue. The sound system, lighting, and acoustics are all state of the art. An inclined floor and elevated stage guarantee superb visibility throughout the house. The three-tiered seating is about as nice as you'll find in any nightclub in the nation, and everything about the Hard Rock is a testimony to the visionary design values dictated on this project by Peter Morton, the international Hard Rock monolith's founder. Two Strip show-pieces fit comfortably in between Thomas & Mack's hugeness and The Joint's comparative intimacy. Booking the likes of Sting or any Jackson currently in town for a post-op, the 15,000-seat **MGM Grand Garden Arena** (part of the MGM Grand Casino Hotel) is the city's plushest venue, with padded seats and cocktail servers in the high-roller sections. The **Aladdin Theater for the Performing Arts** is an older space that, like the rest of Aladdin, is showing some wear and tear at its edges, but which nonetheless is the equal of the concert venues in most American cities. It hosts a popular Broadway Classics series, as well as top VH-1–style acts like Diana Ross and Dwight Yoakam. "Pops" concerts are the specialty of the handsome outdoor **Hills Park Amphitheater** in the real-estate development known as Summerlin; another popular al fresco venue for jazz and "Classics Lite" is at Lorenzi Park's **Sammy Davis, Jr. Festival Plaza** (you didn't think Mr. Bojangles would ever be forgotten, did you?). The city's dozen or so dance companies perform primarily at the **Charleston Heights Arts Center** and the **Reed Whipple Cultural Center**, small auditoriums that lack the more extensive amenities and facilities common in most community performing-arts centers in similar-size cities. Nonetheless, these two venues host a year-round slate of dance productions, from ballet to tap, as well as touring companies. Reed Whipple also serves as one of the homes for the Las Vegas Civic Symphony. The **Artemus Ham Concert Hall**, on the UNLV campus, hosts performances by concert pianists, chamber-music groups, international dance companies, and an occasional touring opera production.

On your toes... At the top of the Vegas performing-arts food chain are this city's thousands of show dancers. Some work nightly in Strip production shows, and some have retired following their glory years toting headdresses around the stages of long-departed places like the Sands and the Dunes. Others have pursued professional careers as dance instructors in the city's many commercial dance academies. Still others fill behind-the-scenes roles as choreographers and coaches for the many commercial dance shows that are cast and rehearsed in Las Vegas before being sent out on international tours. Today, it's common for professional dancers to choose Las Vegas as their home base, not only because of the many production-show employment opportunities at casino showrooms, but also because a drive to television and movie auditions in L.A. takes only five hours. Many of Vegas's transplants, accustomed to supporting the arts in their hometowns, become season subscribers to local dance and theater companies.

If you want an idea of just how integrated into (and integral to) the lives of Las Vegas residents dance is, pick up the phone book and read through the list of more than 50 dance schools and academies teaching the city's kids and adults how to do everything from clogging to two-stepping to tap, jazz, ballet, and ethnic dance. Many programs combine dance instruction with gymnastics, and when you consider that the city's school system teaches both from elementary through high school, it's no wonder that Las Vegas people know more than a little bit about how to conduct themselves on a dance floor, even if they grew up to be CPAs and computer technicians rather than musicians and showgirls. Alas, that doesn't mean they enjoy a tremendous selection of performances by touring metropolitan and international dance companies. But you can find everything from ballet to Broadway-style razzmatazz, folk to funk, all performed by local dancers. Some of the better known, "serious" local dance companies performing regularly and drawing significant audiences are **Las Vegas Civic Ballet**, the area's outlet for classical dance; **Opus Dance Ensemble**, a group made up of professional dancers from the Strip who usually perform their own modern works; **Nevada Dance Theater**, the home of serious modern dance here; and **University Dance Theatre** (at UNLV) bringing up the rear. **Simba Jambalaya Dance Theatre** is known for performing ethnic works. Touring national dance companies such as the Alvin Ailey, Bolshoi Ballet, Ukrainian National Ballet, and New York City Ballet, when they perform in Las Vegas, stage their events at the **Artemus Ham Concert Hall** on the UNLV campus.

Snap, crackle, pop music... As noted in the Nightlife chapter, Las Vegas boasts more than its share of star-powered touring acts. The **Thomas & Mack Center** ropes in the big, publicity-heavy acts like The Cure and Smashing Pumpkins, where the music (which is usually so loud you can't hear it anyway) plays second fiddle to the production pyrotechnics. Las Vegas residents flock every summer to the amphitheater at **Hills Park** in Summerlin for its barrage of evening concerts under the stars, featuring the same caliber of big-name acts playing the Strip's concert venues. The park's bookings emphasize family-friendly musical genres such as folk, jazz, oldies, and light rock acts (Buffy St. Marie, Spyro Gyra, and ex-Herman's Hermit Peter Noone are typical). If you're closer to the Strip and must rely on public transportation, the most readily accessible outdoor-concert space is the **Sammy Davis, Jr. Festival Plaza** at Lorenzi Park, where the city's Cultural and Community Affairs Division presents a summer-long series called **Beyond the Neon**, presenting the likes of jazz great Luther Allison, the American Tap Dance Orchestra, and the Las Vegas Civic Symphony. By far, the city's most popular venue for touring rock, reggae, blues, and alternative bands is **The Joint at the Hard Rock Casino Hotel**. Acts range from the ultra-hip to eternal faves: Chris Isaak, Lyle Lovett, Reggae Sunsplash, Ted Nugent, Boz Scaggs, the Gipsy Kings, and Steely Dan all could be booked into The Joint during one week. This place has become a natural add-on to the performance circuit bands make in L.A. clubs. The **MGM Grand Garden Arena** corrals almost as many top-name, Top-40 performers as the Mack: Gloria Estefan, the Rolling Stones, Sting, Janet Jackson, and Amy Grant are typical of the acts that enjoy more sophisticated surroundings than the Mack's 1980s, industrial/rodeo arena setting provides. The **Aladdin Theatre for the Performing Arts** (inside the Aladdin Casino Hotel) specializes in VH-1 artists and near-nostalgic acts like Dwight Yoakam, Patty LaBelle, Diana Ross, Peter Frampton, Linda Ronstadt, Bobby Womack, and Peter, Paul and Mary. Should you tire of the rowdy and risqué offerings on the Strip, the Las Vegas Hilton (enshrined in local history books as the home of Elvis Presley's 837 consecutive sold-out performances—a record even Wayne Newton and Siegfried & Roy can't touch) hosts occasional concerts in its 1,600-seat **Starlight Theater** by such mellow acts such as The Monkees (a standing-room sell-out, of course), Creedence Clearwater Revisited (no, not revived, just revisited), Lou Rawls, and Nancy Wilson.

Jazzed up... Most of the jazz action in Las Vegas happens at the smaller club venues (see Nightlife), but occasionally there are some larger, concert-style shows. The city's **Beyond the Neon** performing-arts series at Charleston Heights Arts Center, Reed Whipple Cultural Center, Sammy Davis Jr. Festival Plaza, and Cashman Field Theatre includes a steady diet of live jazz music by touring regional and national acts every spring and summer. The main event on the city's jazz calendar is the annual **Las Vegas City of Lights Jazz Festival**, a jazz blowout that continues well into the night at Hills Park's amphitheater in Summerlin. This late-April event's organizers encourage music lovers to bring blankets, baby strollers, lawn chairs, Frisbees, and coolers filled with iced margaritas to enjoy hours of performances by as many as 10 national and local jazz acts such as the Jazz Crusaders, Dave Weckl, and the Gene Redden Quartet. Hills Park also hosts a summertime series, **Concerts at the Hills**, while the **Jazz Under the Stars** series at the **Spring Mountain Ranch State Park Amphitheater** runs nearmonthly performances from May through September, with evening shows spotlighting national acts like Bela Fleck and the Flecktones and Russ Freeman and the Rippingtons. The city's favorite musician is the extraordinarily talented keyboardist Ghalib Ghallab, a wildly popular lounge musician who has played with the likes of Miles Davis and Al Jarreau. His regular afternoon gig at Caesar's Olympic Lounge is a Vegas must-see on anyone's complete itinerary, not just for the quality of the music, but for the strength of his affable personality. He's totally plugged into what's happening in the city, and he's beloved for his charity work. As Al Hirt is to New Orleans, so is Ghalib Ghallab to Las Vegas.

Where to hear Ludwig, Wolfgang, and their pals...

As has occurred recently in many other cities, eminently decent organizations like the Nevada Symphony Orchestra have suffered crippling funding cutbacks and have, in turn, severely curtailed their performance schedules. Las Vegas's orchestras have been hit particularly hard, though. You could blame it on the decline of live music at production shows, which now favor canned backup, but the truth is there never was much demand for egghead music in this bastion of pop-music culture. The situation has become a cutthroat game of musical orchestra chairs: fewer and fewer organizations are competing for increasingly scarce dollars to play in smaller venues. Even the most rabidly loyal locals can't seem to sustain top-level orchestras in a town where the three Bs aren't Bach, Beethoven, and Brahms, but Boobs, Booze, and Blackjack. Of course, just like any other city of a million-plus residents, Las Vegas does have organizations stepping into the role of leading this city's classical music scene, namely the **Las Vegas Civic Symphony**, under the direction of Alan Lewis. The symphony doesn't even have a regular home: Its performances are staged at various venues, ranging from the Sammy Davis Jr. Festival Plaza in Lorenzi Park to Hills Park at Summerlin, the Reed Whipple Cultural Center, and the Artemus Ham Concert Hall. While these places are adequate, all this roaming about from venue to venue isn't exactly conducive to a properly orchestral mindset, and lacks the security necessary for an orchestra to unify and excel in the manner of coevals in cities such as Minneapolis, Albuquerque, and Buffalo. The **Nevada Symphony Orchestra** has been decimated, and today is most prominently known for offering the Las Vegas Pops' Picnic summer outdoor series at Hills Park in Summerlin. It stages occasional winter performances and an annual *Nutcracker* series at Artemus Ham Concert Hall on the UNLV campus. There are also a smattering of chamber-music groups performing with some degree of regularity at such locales as **Summerlin Library Performing Arts Center**, the **Charleston Heights Arts Center**, and the **Clark County Library Theater**. Ensembles such as the Las Vegas Woodwind Quintet, the Silk and Bamboo Ensemble, and Nevada Chamber Symphony attract a loyal following, and offer a welcome respite from the way-over-the-top musical spectaculars on and off the Strip. Of the three, the Silk and Bamboo Ensemble gets the most local attention. If you're here during June be sure to catch at least a few performances at the **Las Vegas Music Festival**, a prominent classical-music event pulling in a national roster of metropolitan-area orchestra professionals as well as top music-school students for 10 days of classes, performances, open rehearsals, and new-music recitals. Most of the festival's performances take place at the **Cashman Field Theatre**, an indoor venue adjacent to the city's minor-league ballpark, Cashman Field. Its wildly popular grand finale concert, with a 90-piece-orchestra conducted

THE ARTS ⟍ THE LOWDOWN

by Evan Christ (a Las Vegas native who founded the festival and who currently teaches at the Liszt Academy in Budapest) is held here. During the festival's 10-day run, chamber groups and soloists also stage a number of performances at the Reed Whipple and Charleston Heights art centers.

The theatah... In a city loaded with production shows, headliner performances, lounge acts, and piano bars, you'd hardly think Las Vegas would be the sort of place where serious theater could have a snowball's chance in hell of surviving. Mostly, you'd be right. Locals and many of this city's legions of newcomer residents are starved for stage presentations featuring neither live animals, topless dancers, nor acrobats. Hence, the enduring popularity of the Aladdin Casino Hotel's **Broadway Classics** series, which lassoes the national touring companies of revival shows such as *Grease, Funny Girl,* and *West Side Story,* as well as the latest efforts of such Broadway institutions as Neil Simon and Andrew Lloyd Webber. With a year-round series that gets into full swing from September to March, the Aladdin almost always features starry-eyed casting of big Hollywood names (mostly from TV). It may not be great art, but in a city where the concept of performance was, not that long ago, equated with full frontal nudity or dirty jokes about adultery, the Aladdin gets a pat on the back for trying. The city's home-grown theater companies put on shows at the **Summerlin Library Performing Arts Center** and the **Charleston Heights Arts Center** for their productions. As is often the case in a city where one form of performance consumes the lion's share of public funding and audience interest (in Vegas, that's dance, of course), the relative scarcity of financial resources has forced the local theater scene into survival mode. That means for the most part a fairly conservative slate of productions. Among Las Vegas's most popular local drama organizations are the **New West Theatre Company** and the **Actors Repertory Theatre**. On occasion, each will present a new play written by a local aspiring playwright, but these companies can little afford to stage a piece that does not generate lots of ticket sales, so New West or Actors Rep will present *To Kill a Mockingbird, Moby Dick,* or *Man of La Mancha* long before they stage *Buried Child* or *American Buffalo.*

One oasis in the theatrical desert is, oddly enough, at UNLV, where the success of the Runnin' Rebels basketball program in the 1980s generated so much income for the school that they're still trying to spend it. Ergo, the **UNLV Theatre Deparment** offers the nation's foremost MFA programs, where emphasis is placed not only on acting but also on design technology, costume design, and scenic arts—all skills in great demand at the production shows and Hollywood shoots taking place around Las Vegas. The college's graduate theatre program presents both a fall and spring performance season, with productions ranging from reworked standards like *A Midsummer's Night Dream* recast as (believe it or not) a magic show, to *A Raisin in the Sun* and original works by winners of the program's biannual "Morton R. Sarett Award," a fairly prestigious national playwrighting competition. Famous graduates of the UNLV theater department include technical pros responsible for staging everything from touring Broadway shows to Strip production extravaganzas to recent Hollywood hits such as *Big* and (of course) *Leaving Las Vegas* and *Casino*.

During the summer months, the quest for cultural action drives Las Vegans into the religious empire of Utah, where just a four-hour hop/skip/speeding ticket away is the summertime **Utah Shakespearean Festival**, held on the campus of Southern Utah University in Cedar City. Its six annual productions take place in three venues—the Adams Shakespearean Theatre (outdoors), the Auditorium Theater (indoors), and the Randall L. Jones Shakespearean Theatre (indoors)—turning this small retirement community into a summertime version of the Globe Theatre during the festival's 10-week season. You can expect strong stage work by seasoned Shakespearean performers, the same theater professionals who, in past years, have worked in Shakespeare hotbeds like Medford, Oregon and Montgomery, Alabama.

For the kids... Children's theater productions can be found, now and again, during evening hours at the **Reed Whipple Cultural Center** and at the **Charleston Heights Arts Center**, both of which pursue a very determined course toward expanding the public's access to fine arts, performing as well as visual. These productions are invariably mainstream material aimed at entertaining kids

THE ARTS & THE LOWDOWN

with edifying messages such as identifying sexual abuse or dealing with neighborhood bullies. Charleston Heights Arts Center's annual **Children's Summer Concert Series** is oriented toward kids age 3 and older, and offers several 7pm performances of pieces such as "Brer Rabbit Tales," as well as readings by local authors of children's books. Super Summer Theater, in the **Spring Mountain Ranch State Park Amphitheater**, has become a very popular series. These family-oriented plays—along the lines of *Jesus Christ Superstar* and *The Pajama Game*—incorporate sophisticated production values, as the acting and backstage work is mostly courtesy of experienced Las Vegas pros wanting to lend their expertise to the community. The park's amphitheater sits high in the Spring Mountains bordering the city's western flank, meaning that the evening temperatures plummet from broil-in-the-nearby-city-furnace to a comfy reheat setting... so bring a sweater.

The Index

Actors Repertory Theatre. This local drama organization primarily stages well-known material—the sort that's familiar to community theater companies everywhere—at the Summerlin Library Performing Arts Center..,. *Tel 702/647–7469. 1771 Inner Circle.*

Aladdin Theater for the Performing Arts. This 7,000-seat venue has been used for more than its share of prizefights and Barbie conventions in years past, but these days its raison d'etre is to serve as a concert hall for oldies acts such as Peter Frampton, revival acts like The Temptations, and an occasional touring musical featured in the Broadway Classics series.... *Tel 702/736–0111. 3667 Las Vegas Blvd. S. Tel 702/736–0250 for Broadway Classics.*

Artemus Ham Concert Hall. By far the city's most acoustically perfect concert facility, Ham Hall is the venue of choice for touring classical musicians, performances of the Las Vegas Civic Symphony, national dance company productions, and recitals.... *Tel 702/895–3801. 4505 S. Maryland Pkwy. (on the UNLV campus).*

Beyond the Neon. During the summer this city-organized performing-arts festival uses four outdoor and indoor venues to present everything from national touring jazz bands to the local symphony orchestra.... *Tel 702/229–6713. 309 S. Third St.*

Cashman Field Theatre. An occasional concert venue for classical and rock concerts, this 1,940-seat facility is operated by the city of Las Vegas.... *Tel 702/386–7200. 850 Las Vegas Blvd. N.*

Charleston Heights Arts Center. This is the busiest and largest of the city's community art centers, and it seems to be used for dance performances, classes, art exhibitions, lectures, and theater productions nearly every night of the year.... *Tel 702/229–6383. 800 S. Brush Ave.*

Children's Summer Concert Series. Has daytime and occasional early evening performances by local and Nevada children's entertainers.... *Tel 702/229–6383. 800 S. Brush Ave.*

Clark County Library Theater. An extensive facility with visual-arts exhibition space and a popular performing-arts theater.... *Tel 702/733–7810. 1401 E. Flamingo Rd.*

Concerts at the Hills. This very popular summer outdoor concert series brings pop, jazz, and blues performers to Summerlin's 1,000-seat ampitheater for early evening, family-friendly shows during the spring and summer months.... *Tel 702/791–4500. Hills Park Amphitheater, 4500 Summerlin Parkway, off U.S. 95 north of Las Vegas.*

Hills Park Amphitheater. When the planned community of Summerlin opened its gates in the late 1980s, it was named after Howard Hughes's grandmother. Developed by the late Hughes's Summa Corporation, Summerlin is only 20 minutes from the Strip, and its outdoor ampitheater is Las Vegas's most popular venue for fair-weather evening concerts during the summer, and daytime concerts during the more temperate months of spring and autumn.... *Tel 702/791–4500 Summerlin Parkway, off U.S. 95 north of Las Vegas.*

Jazz Under the Stars. This summer-long outdoors series of jazz performances are inexpensive opportunities to meet some of the city's most dedicated music fans. Bring a blanket, a cooler, and leave you kids at home, request the concert organizers.... *Tel 702/228–3780.*

The Joint at Hard Rock Casino Hotel. Las Vegas's most sophisticated venue for live music of the amplified variety, The Joint's become a hangout for this city's cool set who crowd around the three bars at the back of the hall, schmoozing their way through whatever action's happening onstage.... *Tel 702/693–5000. 4455 Paradise Rd.*

THE ARTS ⌐ THE INDEX

Las Vegas City of Lights Jazz Festival. Springtime music festivals, wherever they may be, are a wonderful way to announce winter's end. This Las Vegas event, first organized in 1993, draws thousands of music lovers and families to the amphitheater at Hills Park for a day and evening of hot jazz.... *Tel 702/228–3780. Hills Park Amphitheater, 4500 Summerlin Parkway, off U.S. 95 north of Las Vegas.*

Las Vegas Civic Ballet. This apex of the city's classical-dance scene performs at the community's art centers and Ham Hall.... *Tel 702/458–7575. 3265 E. Patrick Lane.*

Las Vegas Civic Symphony. An organization dedicated to the development of young musicians, the civic symphony is a smaller and less expensive alternative to the Nevada Symphony Orchestra, which is why it survives and sort of prospers.... *Tel 702/792–4337. 3667 Las Vegas Blvd. S.*

Las Vegas Music Festival. This 10-day classical-music affair attracts teachers, performers, and students from across the nation, and culminates in a gala concert at the Cashman Field Theater.... *Tel 702/229–6211. 850 Las Vegas Blvd. N.*

MGM Grand Garden Arena. This is Vegas's newest venue for large-scale performances, like concerts by crowd-drawing acts appealing to mature audiences (Elton John, Gloria Estefan) as well as prizefights featuring Mike Tyson and other Lords of the Ring.... *Tel 702/891–7777. 3799 Las Vegas Blvd. S.*

Nevada Dance Theatre. Contemporary dance company with a focus on abstract and new forms of terpsichorean expression.... *Tel 702/732–3838. 1555 E. Flamingo Rd.*

Nevada Symphony Orchestra. In an age of orchestral cutbacks and consolidations, the NSO has managed to survive by sticking to the basics: summer pops concerts and a Christmas-season *Nutcracker*.... *Tel 702/792–4337. 3667 Las Vegas Blvd. S.*

New West Theatre Company. The city's most reliable drama company for interesting performances, some created by local playwrights.... *Tel 702/258–8022. 800 S. Brush Ave.*

THE ARTS ⌒ THE INDEX

Opus Dance Ensemble. Modern-dance company comprised of Strip performers who stage presentations of jazz, ballet and modern dance works, often of their own composition.... *Tel 702/732–9646. 1600 E. Desert Inn Rd., Suite 209D.*

Reed Whipple Cultural Center. This very active community art center is the focal point for much of Las Vegas's local dance scene, and also serves as a primary venue for community theater companies.... *Tel 702/229–6211. 821 Las Vegas Blvd. N.*

Sammy Davis, Jr. Festival Plaza. Easily reached on city buses, Lorenzi Park was once a ritzy resort, but today it's the location of the city's art and historical museums and the Sammy Davis, Jr. Festival Plaza, a concert venue hosting much of the city's popular Beyond the Neon summer performing-arts series.... *Tel 702/229–6358. 3300 W. Washington Ave.*

Simba Jambalaya Dance Theatre. The city's leading ethnic dance company regularly stages performances at local art centers and outdoors in Sammy Davis Jr. Festival Park.... *Tel 702/647–8808. 4229 Beth Avenue.*

Spring Mountain Ranch State Park Ampitheater. One of the most pleasant spots to escape the Las Vegas Valley's withering summer heat is at a theater of music performance at this 500-seat facility in the Spring Mountains.... *Tel 702/875–4141.Spring Mountain State Park is a 20-minute drive from the Strip off W. Charleston Blvd.*

Starlight Theater. Used primarily for performances of *Starlight Express,* this 1,000-seat venue inside the Las Vegas Hilton occasionally books tried-and-true oldies acts.... *Tel 702/ 732–5111. 3000 Paradise Rd.*

Summerlin Library Performing Arts Center. Another of the city's multiuse libraries, this space in Summerlin serves both the visual and performing arts as well as the literary arts.... *Tel 702/256–5111. 1771 Inner Circle.*

Super Summer Theater. This outdoor theater festival stages its family-oriented productions at Spring Mountain Ranch

State Park, high in the Spring Mountains.... *Tel 702/594–7529. At the end of West Charleston Blvd.*

Thomas & Mack Center. Home of the UNLV Runnin' Rebels, this on-campus, industrial-strength arena can cram nearly 19,000 rock, rodeo, or pro-wrestling fans under its roof.... *Tel 702/895–3011. 4505 S. Maryland Pkwy.*

University Dance Theatre. This UNLV dance company stages regular performances in Ham Hall, occasionally with visiting artists.... *Tel 702/895–3827. 4505 S. Maryland Pkwy. (on the UNLV campus). Offices inside Ham Hall, part of the UNLV performing arts department's education and performance complex.*

UNLV Theatre Department. UNLV presents an annual fall and spring season running from early October through April, presenting its plays in both the Judy Bayley Theatre and the Black Box Theatre on campus. Performance times and prices vary, but shows usually get underway at 8pm and ticket prices are generally kept under $10.... *Tel 702/895–3801. 4505 S. Maryland Parkway.*

Utah Shakespearean Festival. This summer performing-arts festival is one of the nation's premier Shakespeare festivals, using three theaters on the campus of a college in Cedar City, Utah.... *Tel 800/752–9849. Cedar City is approximately a 4-hour drive from Las Vegas, on the campus of Southern Utah University.*

THE ARTS ⟋ THE INDEX

spo

rts

5

Vegas may be the nation's
fastest-growing city, but as
a sports town it remains
decidedly minor league.
Sure, there are exceptions,
most notably the big-
league, multimillion-dollar

wagering action taking place inside the city's dozens of casinos. There, before banks of enormous video screens and row upon row of benches resembling press seating at a football stadium, thousands of serious bettors live vicariously as shortstops, point guards, thoroughbred jockeys, and quarterback-eating defensive ends. These wagerers root with a fury and passion that makes Vegas the second-best place to be whenever there's a major battle taking place somewhere in the sports world.

Not coincidentally, professional boxing is the sport most likely to put Vegas at the center of the sports world for any single, glorious night. When a champion's belt is on the line at the MGM Grand Arena, Bally's, or Caesars Palace, high rollers fly into town from around the globe, tickets become extremely hard to find, and scalpers net thousands for ringside seats. Try the relevant casino's box office, or Ticketmaster (tel 702/893–3033). Or if you've been doing some gambling, try wheedling tickets out of your pit boss—they're the ones who carry the comps.

The other major league exception is professional motor sports, which have taken root here in the past few years. Now that the Las Vegas Motor Speedway has opened its state-of-the-art, 25,000-seat track north of town, the big-name NASCAR drivers and even some of the Indy circuit's names are making pit stops in Las Vegas.

Otherwise, sports fans have to acclimate themselves to second-tier action like minor league baseball's Las Vegas Stars, or that once-upon-a-time college basketball powerhouse, the Runnin' Rebels of UNLV. For now, the Vegas area just doesn't have enough potential season ticket–buyers to support a major league team in any sport. One happy result for fans, though, is that tickets can easily be purchased for almost any game right up until the playing of the national anthem.

Meanwhile, for nightcrawlers who want to work out before their nightly rounds, Vegas doesn't lack for indoor options. For those who feel the need to do something like run around outside, during the hottest months the time to exercise outdoors is between 7 and 9pm, between when the sun sets and the neon takes over. Power walkers may head out at as early as six, while joggers might want to wait another hour.

As for the rest of the year (when this town isn't doing its imitation of a kiln), Las Vegas is nothing short of paradise. With such an enticing climate, most every tennis court in town is illuminated for night play, or you can head out to a lit driving range (some of which are even heated during the winter months).

The Lowdown

Where to watch

Go, speed racers... The city's latest advance into big-time sports is the **Las Vegas Motor Speedway** (tel 702/644–4444; 7000 Las Vegas Boulevard N.), now one of the most sophisticated track setups in the West. Located in the northern reaches of Las Vegas Boulevard, out by Nellis Air Force Base (home of the Stealth bomber), LVMS has jumped Vegas' motor sports standing right up into the major leagues. Now it's possible to catch everything from the NASCAR Winston West Series to NHRA jet dragsters, from AMA Superbike motorcycle racing to the rough-and-tumble madness of sprint car racing nearly every night of the week from the speedway's 25,000-seat grandstand. Grab a seat and don't be surprised if you're sitting between an elderly couple wearing Richard Petty T-shirts and a large family digging into their picnic basket. Going to the car races is, in this part of the nation, a democratically demographic experience. Prices for the March-to-October season's races range from $10 to $90, depending on the caliber of the racing and the quality of the seat. Most races start at 7pm, with Friday night's features lasting past midnight.

The lads of winter... Minor League hockey is the brutal end of the pro sports world... a place populated with fresh-faced kids straight off the cornfields of Alberta and horribly scarred vets who have seen all their brighter days fade into their pasts. The **Las Vegas Thunder** (tel 702/798–7825; Thomas & Mack Center, 4505 S. Maryland Pkwy.)—a salute to the desert's summertime thunderstorm action—plays in the International Hockey League, a rough-and-tumble cauldron where teams from places like San Antonio, Orlando, Albuquerque and Sacramento scratch out an existence. The Thunder's season runs from early October through April, and if you want to catch one of their 41 home games head over to the Thomas & Mack Center, plunk down anywhere from $10 to $22, and start hollering.

The boys of simmer... Ya gotta love triple-A baseball. It's played in cozy ballparks, costs just a few bucks for a seat, and the traditional pastoral pleasures of the game are sweetened by syrupy family promotions. The **Las Vegas Stars** (tel 702/474–4000; Cashman Field, 850 Las Vegas Blvd. N.), are the top minor-league club of the San Diego Padres, a franchise that every decade or so manages to plug together a good enough lineup to power it into the National League playoffs. The Stars are a decent enough team if you need a baseball fix while in Vegas. They play in in the Southern Division of the triple-A Pacific Coast League, along with teams like the Albuquerque Dukes and the Tucson Toros. The team's home field is the easy-to-reach, 10,000-seat Cashman Field, part of a city-operated facility that also houses a convention center and a concert theater (see The Arts). It's hot at Cashman, usually 100 degrees or more when the first pitch is thrown at about 7pm, but get there early in case Huey Lewis or some other visiting Vegas performer is singing the national anthem. Other welcome extras in the 1983 park are an air-conditioned restaurant behind home plate, and, of course, the stadium martinis. And if you show up on a promo night, you might walk out with anything from a coupon for a free haircut to a water bottle for your bike. The Stars' season spans from April through Labor Day and tickets run from $3 down the foul lines to $8 for a place right behind the dugout.

Hoop dreams... During the winter months, the only big-time local sports action is on the UNLV campus, where the **Runnin' Rebels** still give their best shot at running with the best of the NCAA. There have been no national championships since Larry (Grandmama) Johnson and Coach Jerry (The Shark) Tarkanian left town, but that run-and-gun, Oakland Raiders-type outlaw history still boosts the local image. The Rebels, who play just a few miles from the Strip at Thomas & Mack Center (tel 702/895–3900; 4505 S. Maryland Parkway), take on the rest of the NCAA from September through March. Tickets aren't hard to come by. Prices range from $10 to $18.

Where to play

Playing the odds... Most of the larger casino hotels have what they call "sportsbooks," gambling facilities where bettors can wager on anything from Japanese thoroughbred racing to the Super Bowl. The great thing about the sportsbooks is that they all have video screens where you can check out the Sunday football games, NBA games, etc., and some of them are set up to be inviting lounges where you can order drinks, sandwiches, and even place keno bets while you're cheering on whatever team you've backed. Some of the best sportsbooks are at the **Las Vegas Hilton** (tel 702/732–5111; 3000 Paradise Rd.), which is huge, dark, and loaded with enormous video screens. **MGM Grand**'s (tel 702/894–7111; 3900 Las Vegas Blvd. S.) sportsbook isn't as serious or as dark a place as the Hilton. But part of its appeal is that the operation's many good fast food joints are conveniently nearby. If you're out on the Boulder Strip be sure to drop in at the **Boulder Station** sportsbook (tel 702/432–7777; 4111 Boulder Hwy.), a place worth visiting just to check out the serious faces of the professional sports gamblers who pack this place whenever there's a big game, race or fight happening.

Up to par... If you've just got to get out and hit a few golf balls in the middle of the night, there are a couple of 24-hour driving ranges worth checking out. The **Green Valley Golf Range** (tel 702/434–4300; Corner of Warm Springs & Stephanie) is an outdoors range with 94 shaded tees that are warmed by electric heaters during cold winter nights. **Star Golf Lounge** (tel 702/247–4653; 3000 Meade Ave.) has a smaller and less elaborate indoor setup (nets catch your drives), along with the typical Vegas trappings of a video poker bar scene. There's a driving range and a lighted, par-3 course at **Angel Park Golf Course** (tel 702/254–4653; 100 S. Rampart Blvd., closes at 10pm). Closest to the Strip is the **Las Vegas Hilton Country Club** (tel 702/796–0016; 1911 E. Desert Inn Rd.; last tee time is 6pm during the summer months; $125 for guests,

SPORTS $\bigcirc$ THE LOWDOWN

$145 for non-guests), a tournament-caliber course whose driving range and putting green close down at 8pm. And if your golf fun revolves around the putt-putt course, keep in mind that right on the west side of I-15 there's an 18-hole miniature golf course at **Scandia Family Fun Center** (tel 702/364–0070; 2900 Sirius Ave.; open until midnight weekends, until 11pm weeknights).

Other racquets... Many of of the Strip's casino hotels have a few tennis courts that stay open into the early evening, but don't expect to find any action down on Glitter Gulch, where the casino hotels were established decades ago, before guests started arriving with their rackets. **Bally's** (tel 702/739–4111; 3645 Las Vegas Blvd. S.; open until 8pm; $10 for guests, $15 for everyone else) is a choice Strip tennis mecca, with eight outdoor composition courts. For fans of the ghost of Elvis, who like to play now and then, The **Las Vegas Hilton** (tel 702/739–4111; 3000 Paradise Rd.; open until 8pm; free to hotel guests, off-limits to all others) boasts six outdoor composition courts.

Midnight sweat... All those hardbodies you see prancing around in the casino hotel production shows or dancing in the city's bars and lounges have a decided advantage in their battle to remain ogle-worthy: Where else do the health clubs commonly stay open 24 hours, allowing stairclimbers and pec-builders to do their sweaty routines while the rest of the West is getting a good night's rest?

Though many of the Strip's casino hotels maintain their own health clubs, such operations tend to keep virtual bankers' hours (actually, about 8am to 5pm) and their day rates—$5 to $15 for hotel guests—aren't much better than the all-nighters'.

The 24-hour club closest to the Strip (within walking distance of the Mirage, Circus Circus, Treasure Island, etc.) is the **Las Vegas Sporting House** (tel 702/733–8999; 3025 Industrial Rd.; $15 for a day pass, $50 for a weeklong pass). It doesn't look like much from the outside, but this 65,000-square-foot health club not only has the latest possible in workout equipment, it has it in the dozens. You want Nautilus? You want Cybex? You want Stairmaster? The Sporting House has enough machines so that you'll never have to wait on line for the privilege of tightening those buns.

SPORTS ⟨ THE LOWDOWN

You can't go more than a mile or two from the Strip without running into another 24-hour health club. The **Family Fitness Center** chain has a club hard by the Strip (tel 702/641–2222; 2605 S. Eastern Ave; $10 for a day pass, $25 for a weeklong pass) to cater to the all-night, I-gotta-do-it-now crowd, while the **Las Vegas Athletic Club** (tel 702/734–5822; 1070 E. Sahara Ave.; $10 for a day pass, $25 for a weeklong pass) also takes the flab-never-sleeps philosophy to heart at its Sahara Avenue location. No matter which of these two franchises you choose, you'll find each club equipped with locker rooms, new fitness equipment, aerobics classes (but don't count on finding a step class at 3am), along with racquetball courts, steam rooms, swimming pools and saunas. Serious bar-busters will love the fact that **Gold's Gym** keeps its two locations open 24 hours (tel 702/877–6966, 2610 S. Decatur Blvd.; tel 702/451–4222; 3750 E. Flamingo Rd.), with the location on South Decatur being closest to the Strip. A competitor, **World Gym** (tel 702/435–5646; 4754 S. Eastern Ave.), is also open 24 hours. It's a longer drive from Las Vegas Boulevard, but much closer to the casino hotels along the Boulder Strip. Day passes at either gym are $10, with weeklong passes going for $35.

On the run... Most people's idea of a place to go for a run involves trees, green grass and a jogging trail. The only place which even remotely meets this description close to the Strip is on **the campus of UNLV** (off Tropicana Boulevard; park near The Thomas & Mack Center, which you can't miss) although if you're not a student, you could get asked for ID. Your other option is running in and out of the neon jungle, parallel to the Strip. Although you see the occasional kamikaze jogger running through the crowds on the Strip, the north-south streets such as Industrial Road on the west side of the Strip, and Koval Lane and Paradise Road on the east side, are favorites of tourists who are staying in the hotels and need a less crowded sidewalk to run along.

Ice capades... Not even the joy of escaping into a refrigerated climate for a few hours of ice skating fun has escaped the imaginative reaches of this desert city's entrepreneurs. For whatever reason, some folks just can't fight the urge to play ice hockey or emulate Tonya Harding, even if nature's putting on a roaring, 110-

degree furnace outside the rink's doors. The largest and most mind-boggling skating facility in the area is the one at the **Santa Fe Hotel & Casino** in the north end of the city (tel 702/658–4991; 4949 Rancho Drive, Rancho at U.S. 95; open until 10pm Wed, until 1am Fri–Sat; $5 for adults, $4 for kids, skate rentals $2). There's something surreal about walking into the Santa Fe on a blazing summer day, wandering around the casino's far reaches to the skating rink's doors, and pulling them open to find 12 teenagers on the ice banging slapshots off the goalies with a midwinter vengeance. Yes, it's a refrigerated haven for those who find the desert heat unbearable, but it doesn't take long for the arena's 55-degree air temperature to bore a hole right through the sole of your sandals.

Downhill gambler... If you're in Las Vegas between Thanksgiving and mid-March, the absolutely coolest nighttime fun you can have is skiing or snowboarding in the Toiyabe National Forest's alpine ski area, the **Las Vegas Ski and Snowboard Resort** (tel 702/878–5465; Hwy. 156, approximately 50 miles from the Strip; open until 10pm; lift tickets are $27 for adults, $20 for kids.). With its 8,500-foot elevation, 1,000 vertical feet of runs, three chairlifts, and night skiing, this place could offer the perfect start to a night that could only happen in Vegas. During the summer months, the ski area's $4 chairlift rides are a great way to beat Las Vegas' heat. Nobody's going to confuse this ski area with Jackson Hole, but it's not a bad alternative if you're here and just have to clear out your head by pushing some powder.

Waterworlds... Here in the Mojave Desert, it's swimming pool weather from Easter until Thanksgiving—unless you're a tourist from some rugged northern climate, and then it's swimming pool weather even while the rest of Vegas is huddled in front of their video fireplaces.

The casino hotels usually close down their pools during the coldest months, December through February. If you don't want to miss your laps, check out the heated pools in the health clubs (see "Midnight Sweat," above). During the rest of the year, poolside action is an integral function of the Vegas experience. Knowing this, the pools at casino hotels stay open until 10pm, though sneaking in for a quiet dip at 3am seems to be some sort of tradition.

Most of the hotels added pool areas as after-thoughts—capitulations to the demands of guests managers would rather see glued to the screen of a video poker machine all hours of the day and night. At such places, the pool area never gets the attention lavished on lounges and restaurants (i.e., the money-making ends of the operation). Fortunately, there are exceptions. The **Tropicana Resort & Casino** (tel 800/634–4000; 3801 Las Vegas Boulevard S.) has what's widely considered to be the city's nicest pool, with a decidedly tropical flair and enough room that everyone can spread out under the palm trees without bumping into each other. The similarly lush environment at the **Flamingo Hilton** (tel 800/732–2111; 3555 Las Vegas Boulevard S.), has some novel touches, such as a water tube course for kids, waterfalls and an aviary with—you guessed it—pink flamingoes!

For more water fun, local folks love going to **Wet 'n' Wild** (tel 702/734–0088; 2601 Las Vegas Boulevard S.; open daily until 11pm; June–August, until 8pm May–Sept; $21.95 for ten years and over, $15.95 for kids ages 3 to 9, $10.95 for adults 55 and older), which is not only Las Vegas's largest and best-equipped water park, but is also located right on the Strip. This sprawling, 24-acre amusement park attracts huge crowds, especially families who spread out picnic blankets on the broad, green lawns. Definitely check out the Bomb Bay, a twisting water tunnel, as well as the Blue Niagara water slide and the volleyball action by the park's Beach Club. Wet 'n' Wild also hooks up regularly with one of the local rock radio stations to stage special promotional nights featuring bands, T-shirt giveaways and reduced cost admissions.

Bowling... The pro bowlers tour has long made an annual stop at the **Showboat Casino Hotel** (tel 702/385–9123; 2800 E. Fremont St.; open 24 hours; $2.05 per game for adults, $1.55 for children up to the age of 18). This state-of-the-art, 106-lane bowling center is the sort of place pros like swooping down on for tournaments, and local families feel welcome on weekends. North of town, the **Santa Fe Casino Hotel** (tel 702/658–4900; 4949 Rancho Dr.; open till 11pm; $8.50 per hour) has a video arcade, child-care room and even a Ben & Jerry's outside of its 60-lane, spanking new facility. Closest to the Strip is the **Gold**

Coast Casino Hotel's (tel 702/367–4700; 4000 W. Flamingo Rd.; open 24 hours; $1.90 per game) 72-lane bowling center on the casino's second floor. (For video games and amusement parlors, see Hanging Out.)

Start your engines... Mindful that anyone who can sit for hours at the Las Vegas Motor Speedway probably would like to get his or her own hands on the wheel of a race car, several Las Vegas amusement parks feature mini-tracks where anyone can work that jet-fuel jones out of their system. The best of these is the **Las Vegas Mini Gran Prix** (tel 702/259–7000; 1401 N. Rainbow Rd., exit 82A off U.S. 95; open until midnight, until 11pm Sun; $4 for a five-minute go-cart ride, $17.50 for a five-ride pass), located in the northwest part of the city and featuring a sophisticated, four-track facility with everything from go-slow carts for younger kids to "full size," Indy-like gran prix carts for adults. There's even a banked track with NASCAR-style go-carts.

Open a bit later (until 1am, Mon–Sat) is **Competition Gran Prix** (tel 702/431–7223; 2980 S. Sandhill, Boulder Highway exit off U.S. 95), which is located near the Boulder Strip and offers a relative bargain at $3.50 for a six-minute ride. The three-track layout here is a bit more stripped-down, with an emphasis on serious driving. **Scandia Family Fun Center** (tel 702/364–0070; 2900 Sirius Ave., between Spring Mountain and Sahara off-ramps from Interstate 15; open until 1am, until midnight Sun; $3.95 for a five-minute loop) is the go-cart facility closest to the Strip, but it's also the slowest and most boring of the three inside the city.

Cue tips... This being a top spot for hustlers of all sorts, you won't be surprised to learn that Vegas is home to a mess of all-night pool halls. One of my favorites is **Pink-E's Fun Food & Spirits** (tel 702/252–4666; 4170 S. Valley View Blvd.; 50¢ per game; open 24 hours), where even the sharks have to play on pink felt. Pink-E's maintains a fifties diner decor, has lots of kitschy Elvis-meets-Route 66 memorabilia strewn about, and on weekends features some fairly lively bands on its small stage. Fortunately, the place is large enough that if the band's crankin' on one end of the house, and you're shooting a few racks on the other end, you won't have your ears blasted by some maniac on stage doin' the rock 'n' roll hoochie koo.

A more serious regard for the game is upheld at the **Lion's Den** (tel 702/735–7600; 1325 E. Flamingo Rd.; 50¢ per game; open 24 hours), which has nearly 70 pool tables arranged on the floor of what was once was a strip-mall supermarket. This 24-hour operation is a serious shooter's dream, with green felt tables, normal-volume rock on the sound system, cheap drafts at the bar and respectful people playing at the tables. There's also a room in back that's Vegas's best place for serious dart throwers. Come to the Lion's Den if you want to improve your game or just entertain a guest, not if you just want to fight for your right to party. There are other places for that, namely Pink-E's.

Hiking... The few hours bracketing sunset may seem like an odd period of time to head out on a hike, but here in the desert Southwest, folks have to plan their summer mountain excursions around the heat. As a result, early evening hikes are a traditional way for locals to get in touch with mother nature. The city's proximity to the Toiyabe National Forest, nestled inside the Spring Mountain Range flanking Las Vegas' western boundary, means you'll have easy access to anything from scaling 11,918-foot Mt. Charleston to taking more relaxed hikes in the Red Rock Canyon National Conservation Area. This high desert oasis offers several trails, ranging from the relatively short and easy 2 1/2-mile cruise on Icebox Canyon Trail to the more difficult Turtlehead Peak 5-mile climb. Just 15 miles from the city's western limits, Red Rock Canyon is the region's most popular draw for hikers, rock climbers, mountain bikers, and backwoods campers. The **U.S. Bureau of Land Management** maintains a **visitors center** at Red Rock Canyon (tel 702/363–1921; 15 miles west of the Strip at the end of West Charleston Boulevard). A number of specialized outdoor-excursion businesses catering to mountain bikers trips, rock climbers, and just plain hikers are located in Las Vegas, such as **Bike & Hike Tours** (tel 702/596–2953) and **Sky's the Limit** (tel 702/363–4533). Be sure to consult one of the above before setting out on your own. And don't stay out too late. The temperature drops fast, and it's all too easy to plunge over a precipice in the dark.

hangi

ng out

Until Bugsy Siegel hit
town, Las Vegas really
came up craps in the
attractions department.
But then Bugsy opened the
Flamingo's doors in 1947,
setting off a building

boom that hasn't quit. According to the city's news bureau, Las Vegas is now America's fastest-growing city. Rove beyond the Strip and downtown, of course, and Las Vegas's urban sprawl reflects an astonishing dearth of imagination. A prefab Sun Belt nightmare, it seems to have no neighborhoods with any ethnic, historic, or even horticultural value whatsoever. But hey, who needs neighborhoods when you've got the Strip? Who needs culture when you've got casinos? Those are where most of the action concentrates in Las Vegas, and even if you're not gambling or taking in a show, the casino hotels still have a host of attractions to suck visitors into their Technicolor vortex.

If you fly into Vegas after sunset, you'll see it at once from the air—that mass of neon signage and spotlit megahotel exteriors looks like a Liberace-ized version of Ronald Reagan's "shining city on the hill"—the American dream gone unhinged, where bigger is better, and illusion is everything. The Strip's aggressive, "hey, look at this!" attitude hits you right between the eyes. I'll clue you into a handful of cafes and coffeehouses-cum-art galleries where you can find some refuge from the ubiquitous mayhem of glitz. But on the whole, you can't take the Vegas out of Las Vegas.

Sometimes merely cruising The Strip (preferably in a convertible) is all you need to have a good time. After all, what other skyline in the world can claim an Egyptian pyramid, the Emerald City, Camelot, the Empire State Building, and an imperial Roman palace? Las Vegas out-Disneys Disney for sheer imagination and excess—no wonder it's turning into one of America's favorite theme parks. The theme park comparison isn't just a metaphor, either; every major casino hotel offers some sort of tourist attraction, whether it's cruising the Nile at the Luxor, viewing an erupting volcano at the Mirage, or dodging gunfire during a sea battle between a British man-of-war and a pirate ship at Treasure Island. Even the shops (where else to spend your winnings?) re-create some theme environment, the most (in)famous being the faux-Greek Forum Shops at Caesars Palace.

Off the Strip, Las Vegas's other attractions tend to have the same kind of hard-'n'-shiny, calling-all-sinners quality: Arcades, tattoo parlors, sex shops…. Despite all that tourist bureau hype about Las Vegas becoming a "family destination," the number of XXX newspapers available on "the Track" (hookerese for the Strip) is a pretty good indication of what Las Vegas is still all about. Unlike Disney World, Vegas World doesn't have a sanitized Magic Kingdom Main Street. But then, that's what a lot of people like about it.

The Lowdown

Surfing the neon wave... Hoover Dam, whose turbines provide the megawattage driving Vegas's air conditioners, hydraulic lifts, and one-armed bandits, bathes this city in cheap electricity, which casino owners squander recklessly on gazillion-watt signage. Las Vegas is a neon salesman's wet dream: It's flat, has practically no humidity, and is virtually unhampered by zoning laws. When the Sahara sports a 23-story-neon sign, the Rio counters with a neon fireworks display that's not only taller and wider, but also boasts more colors than a kickline's feathery headdresses. In a town that builds everything to absurd dimensions (where else are 3,000-room hotels the norm?), the competition for your attention is fierce. And what better way to transfix tourists than by slapping up miles of neon glass tubing?

Ever the visionary, Bugsy Siegel single-handedly brought Vegas into neon fame when he commissioned a pair of 80-foot neon highball glasses, complete with pink fizzies inside, for the Flamingo Hotel. Today, that same hotel is called the **Flamingo Hilton** (3555 Las Vegas Blvd. S.), and though the neon cocktails are, regrettably, a thing of the past, the current humongous neon sign is a riotous explosion of pinkness. Inspired by the fanned tails of peacocks, but using a half-dozen or so shades of pink neon (hot, wild, peachy, or powder-puff), the Flamingo Hilton's curving facade towers 50 feet above the casino's Las Vegas Boulevard entrance.

Every casino hotel along the Strip today has a huge sign incorporating neon, electric lights, steel, and whatever, but the wildest is the 25-story explosion of neon just off the Strip at the **Rio Suites Casino Hotel** (3700 W. Flamingo Rd.). Imagine Carmen Miranda's headgear on super-steroids and you've got the general idea. Just as cool, if nowhere near as colorful, is the 100-foot guitar pro-jecting from the roof of the **Hard Rock Cafe** (corner of Paradise and E. Harmon Rds.)—just in case you didn't already understand the Hard Rock's raison d'être. The honors for tallest neon sign go to the **Las Vegas Hilton** (3000 Paradise Rd.), though it's visually boring—a sort of rectangular scoreboard in the sky. Far better is the sign at the **Stardust** (3000 Las Vegas Blvd. S.), a flood of rain-bow-hued light that evokes the Vegas of days gone by, without looking outdated.

If you really want the old Vegas look, head downtown, where the earlier casino hotels congregated. The city's most famous neon sign is **Vegas Vic**, that cig-puffing, arm-waving cowboy who for decades welcomed visitors to the now-closed Pioneer Club on Fremont Street, between First and Main. (Right across the street is **Vegas Vickie**, a neon goddess who kicks her gams from atop the Girls of Glitter Gulch.) Though he's still lit up, Vic, like the rest of Vegas, is waiting to see what destiny casino magnate Steve Wynn, who bought the Pioneer Club, chooses for him. Meanwhile, Vic hangs around above the **Fremont Street Experience**, a vaulted, steel canopy spangled with light bulbs that runs along Fremont between Main Street and Las Vegas Boulevard. The Fremont Street Experience isn't neon, but in some ways, it out-neons neon: it's a synchro-nized light show using more than two million colored bulbs and 540,000 watts of sound. Using light bulbs the same way a television screen uses pixels to create a video image, the Experience's five-block long "screen" presents moving pictures—everything from a cheesecake lineup of dancing showgirls to a tropical rain forest to cheesy patri-otic scenes of acrobatic jet fighters and a waving American flag. Artistically, it may be a loser, but it's a technical KO. (Just goes to show what the city of Las Vegas does with the odd extra $70 million—some cities build subways; Vegas builds tourist attractions.) One of the city's top freebies, in a city where freebies are a way of life, this 10-minute show takes place every half-hour between 9pm and midnight; all the Fremont Street casinos helpfully shut off their lights during the Experience's 10-minutes-of-fame routine. (It's in their interests to help out, if the Experience draws visi-tors away from the Strip and back to Fremont Street.) The best viewing place is at the Las Vegas Boulevard end, because the images are programmed to move from Main Street toward Las Vegas Boulevard.

Jaw-dropping views... For sheer height, nothing matches the vertiginous look down at Las Vegas from the top of the observation deck of the **Stratosphere** (2000 Las Vegas Blvd. S.; $7 adults, $5 children). Glass panels surrounding the observation deck slant outward from the 1,149-foot-high tower's center; lean out over the panels and you can stare straight down upon the dizzying neon glare of Las Vegas, far, far below. You can also gaze down at commercial airliners flying in and out of McCarran Airport, or just gape in slack-jawed wonder at the Strip, which after sunset resembles a line of sequined showgirls. But here's a well-kept secret: you needn't pay for the privilege of enjoying a great view of the Strip, or the rest of Las Vegas, for that matter. From the top level of almost any parking garage along the Strip, you can get an open-air, unobstructed vista. Look past the less-glitzy backside of the nearest casino hotel and you can see all the other Strip showplaces spread out in their gaudy splendor. Among the most impressive panoramas are those from the top of the self-park lots behind **Caesars Palace** (3570 Las Vegas Blvd. S.) and **Treasure Island** (3300 Las Vegas Blvd. S.). Or, if you want an even more sweeping view, drive away from the Strip to **Sam's Town Hotel and Casino** (5111 Boulder Highway), where the top level of the parking lot gives you a vista of the Strip as well as all of the city's east and north sides. Nothing matches the view from **Sunrise Mountain** (which some locals refer to as Frenchman's Mountain), a spectacular natural perch located 20 minutes from the Strip at the far eastern end of Lake Mead Boulevard. Sunrise or sunset, or even in the middle of the night, this is the place to appreciate the spectacle of what man hath wrought in the Las Vegas Valley.

Intense lobbying... One of the most unforgettable experiences in this city comes absolutely free of charge: casing out the public areas of the casino hotels. Lobby-hopping is a must for anyone visiting Las Vegas for the first time. The Strip's newest casino hotels have poured tens of millions of dollars into signature public spaces, the aesthetic equivalent of whacking you over the head with a 2-by-4. Even the most competitive hotels recognize the value of encouraging tourists to wander from one to the other, gaping at the wild facades and interiors. Start at the cluster of casino hotels on Las Vegas Boulevard at Tropicana Avenue—the Excalibur; New York, New York; the Luxor; the Tropicana; and the

MGM Grand, all of which are linked by elevated skywalks across Las Vegas Boulevard. Begin down at the **Excalibur** (tel 702/597–7777, 3850 Las Vegas Blvd. S.), a beautifully illuminated, turreted medieval-style castle that looks like it was beamed into the Vegas Valley by the Wizard of Oz. Like Caesars Palace and Bally's, it has a moving sidewalk several hundred feet long, on which pedestrians glide from the Strip to the casino entrance. As if the moat, drawbridge, 265-foot bell towers, turrets, and battlements of the Excalibur weren't enough, the interior carries the theme to absurd extremes with sconces, tapestries, and wandering minstrels, jesters, knights errant, and assorted lords and ladies of the court, all assiduously wishing guests, "Have a royal day." **New York, New York** (tel 702/740–6969, 3790 Las Vegas Blvd. S.) is lorded over by a half-scale version of the Statue of Liberty, who—in the Vegas version of New York geography—graces the entrance to the Empire State Building (here only 47 stories tall, though). Over at the **MGM Grand** (tel 702/891–1111, 3799 Las Vegas Blvd. S.), the entrance to the Hollywood-esque interior is dominated by the MGM studio's logo, blown up to mega-proportions—a gold lion's head with jaws open wide so you can stroll right in (just in case you're wondering how the early Christians felt in the Roman arenas). The **Tropicana** (tel 702/739–2222, 3801 Las Vegas Blvd. S.) has the least "wow" factor, but the most kitschy charm of any of its neighbors; the confusing entrance looks like a New England fishing village, but soon it gives way to the tropical, Ricky Ricardo-meets-Bugsy Siegel setting you'd expect. The **Luxor** (tel 702/262–4000, 3900 Las Vegas Blvd. S.) is a few minutes' walk south from the Excalibur, but it really has to be included on the same itinerary—you've just gotta step inside the world's largest (30 stories tall) pyramid, made of steel, glass, and concrete, and gawk at the realistic-looking Egyptiana spread around the interior. It even has an "archeological dig," complete with various replicas of Egyptian antiquities, fronting the banks of the "Nile."

Of course, there's nothing else quite like the melange of pseudo-classical statuary installed at **Caesars Palace** (tel 702/731–7110, 3750 Las Vegas Blvd. S.), where you can gawk at a garish 20-foot image of Caesar himself, an enormous Apollo, and an indoor version of the Trevi fountain. Caesars's grounds are liberally littered, indoors and out, with replicas of famed statues like the *Winged Victory* and Michelangelo's *David* and *Bacchus*—it's about as close to a permanent art museum as you're likely to find in Vegas. Its equal in the can-you-top-this-kitsch category is **Circus Circus** (tel 702/734–0410, 2880 Las Vegas Blvd. S.), immortalized by Hunter S. Thompson in *Fear and Loathing in Las Vegas* for its bizarre collection of acrobats and bikers trapped in glass balls like rats in a wheel, transforming the public spaces into a three-ring big top for suckers born every minute. It's also a hoot to see the 90-foot-high atrium lobby of **The Mirage** (tel 702/791–7111, 3400 Las Vegas Blvd. S.), filled with 60-foot palms that vault like the arches at Chartres, orchids and banana trees that waft more perfume than the Polynesian women hawking their wares in the Tahiti airport, plus the requisite cascading waterfalls and sparkling lagoons. Just behind the registration desk, a leviathan 53-foot-long, 20,000-gallon aquarium replicates a stunning coral reef, where the passing parade o' fish includes gliding rays and menacing sharks.

Best outdoor spectacle... At **Treasure Island** (tel 702/894–7111, 3300 Las Vegas Blvd. S.), the outdoor show overpowers the interior decor, with a complete naval battle staged every 90 minutes (until 11:30pm Fri–Sat, until 10pm Sun–Thur). Set in a theatrical re-creation of Buccaneer Bay, the village in the hotel's namesake Robert Louis Stevenson classic, a titanic sea battle between a British frigate and a pirate ship is waged, including cannon fire across the lagoon, various explosions, and a sinking ship (best of all, the pirates always win). It even comes complete with B-movie dialogue: The British captain opens the salvo with, "I order you brigands to lay down your arms and receive a Marine boarding party" (sounds like something you might hear in a gay bar, huh?). Inevitably, passing drivers slow down to watch, and soon traffic on Las Vegas Boulevard has ground to a halt in both directions. Keep track of Treasure Island's show schedule if you need to get anywhere in a hurry at night.

For the kid in us all... Ever since some of Las Vegas's casino hotel operators started angling for a slice of the nation's family vacation market, this city has assiduously promoted itself as another Magic Kingdom, smack dab in the Mojave Desert. Yeah, and if you believe that, maybe the New York, New York hotel has a piece of the Brooklyn Bridge to sell you. Certainly some casino hotels

(Circus Circus, Excalibur, Treasure Island, and the Monte Carlo) have staked their reputations on being "family friendly," but others—the Mirage, Rio, Caesars Palace, Hard Rock Hotel, and Riviera—frankly don't give a damn (wonder why—could it be because you have to be 21 to enter a casino?), and defiantly market themselves as "adult-friendly" operations.

Still, the Strip's mega-hotels do offer miniature theme parks galore, with features directed to adults as much as children. At the MGM Grand (tel 702/891–1111, 3799 Las Vegas Blvd. S.), **MGM Grand Adventures** (open until 10pm, $17 adults, $12 children) does its considerable best to out-Epcot Walt by creating eight movie-set-like "areas" on 33 acres: Casablanca Plaza; Asian Village; Tumbleweed Gulch; New Orleans Street; Olde England Street; Salem Waterfront; French Street; and New York Street. Like Epcot, it's smoothly sugar-coated—there are no Bourbon Street drunks in this New Orleans, no witch-burnings in this Salem, no snotty waiters in this France. But there is one thrilling ride: Grand Canyon Rapids, which combines elements of a log flume ride with round bumper boats big enough to seat 10. Then there's the disappointing Backlot River Tour, which parades you past a superficial series of scenes featuring swamp creatures, Vietnam War chopper battles, and the like, with incongruous tour guides like Betty Boop. At Circus Circus (tel 702/734–0410, 2880 Las Vegas Blvd. S.), the pink-domed AdventureSphere contains **Grand Slam Canyon** (open until midnight, $13.95 adults, $9.95 kids), a 5-acre indoor amusement park replete with 140-foot peaks and a cascading 90-foot version of Havasupai Falls. Of its two rides, the Canyon Blaster roller coaster is fantastic, the log flume so-so, but the main point here is the cool climate—it's an air-conditioned magnet for every kid visiting Las Vegas. At the **Luxor** (tel 702/262–4000, 3900 Las Vegas Blvd. S.), you can actually float down the replica Nile, touring replicas of the ancient wonders of Egypt—just think of it as the Pharaoh's own Circle Line cruise.

Where to lose your lunch... The **Canyon Blaster**, a double-loop, double-corkscrew roller coaster at Circus Circus's Grand Slam Canyon (see "For the kid in us all," above) is currently the Strip's best ride. But in Las Vegas, there's always somebody ready to outdo the best, and in this case it's the New York, New York casino hotel (tel 702/740–6969, 3790 Las Vegas Blvd. S.). When New York, New York opens its doors in early 1997, its **Manhattan Express** roller coaster (open until midnight; $5) will careen across the casino's ersatz Manhattan skyline at 60 miles per hour, plunging through a heart-twisting dive with an outside loop. Atop the awesome tower of the Stratosphere (tel 702/380–7777, 2000 Las Vegas Blvd. S.), the **Let it Ride High Roller** roller coaster (open Sun–Thur until 1am, Fri–Sat until 2am; $5) circumnavigates the observation deck at nearly 30mph, dipping and diving along 865 feet of steel track. But if you really want to test your guts, try the Strat's **Big Shot** (open until 1am; $5), which is unlike any other thrill ride in the world. This rocket of a ride sends you up *above* the 1,149-foot tower (that's more than 100 stories tall, for you city folks), blasting you at 45mph up 160 vertical feet of nothing but steel track, while you sit harnessed to a padded seat. It's absolutely petrifying; you get the distinct impression that you're headed on a one-way death trip to Mars. You'll also be groping for solid ground after sampling the dizzying flight simulator in part one of the otherwise mediocre **Secrets of the Pyramid** ride at the Luxor (tel 702/262–4000; 3900 Las Vegas Blvd. S.; open until 11pm; $5); by early 1997, the Luxor should also have finished upgrading the Nile river cruise to a bona fide thrill ride. Among the relatively tame flumes and bumper boats at the **Wet 'n' Wild** water park (tel 702/737–3819; 2600 Las Vegas Blvd. S.; in summer open until 11pm, $21.95 adults; prices and times vary at other times of the year), you can churn up a tidal wave in your bloodstream with Banzai Banzai, a double-slide water coaster where riders can race side by side, while Bomb Bay is like a bungee jump without the cord: a 76-foot vertical water slide whose bottom literally drops out, dunking the daredevil into the drink. By far the scariest of all Vegas roller coaster rides is the **Desperado** at Buffalo Bill's Resort & Casino (tel 702/382–1111; 40 miles south of Las Vegas on I-15, in Stateline, NV; open weeknights until 10pm, weekends until midnight; $4). Not for the faint of heart, Desperado hurtles riders along more than 6,000 feet of track at 80mph, hurls them down a 225-foot vertical drop at a 65-degree angle (you'll feel 3 Gs of force crunching against your rib cage), then throws them through a few double loops and twists before setting their feet back onto terra firma. BYOBB:

Bring your own barf bag. After the Desperado chills your spine, the only comparable thrill left is the skydiving simulator at **Flyaway** (tel 702/731–4768; 200 Convention Center Dr.; open until midnight; $27), which zips you into a padded suit so that you can suspend yourself in mid-air over a giant propeller for half an hour. Don't worry, a steel mesh floor saves you from becoming hamburger.

Don't know much about history... Has anyone at the Convention and Visitors Bureau considered promoting Las Vegas for history-class field trips? The **World of Caesar** at Caesars Palace (tel 702/731–7110, 3750 Las Vegas Blvd. S.) provides a surprisingly detailed depiction of a Roman temple, as well as the Forum. Caesars is truly nondenominational (especially when it comes to the pagan rituals enacted at the Cleopatra's Barge nightclub): It also offers the Brahma Shrine, a re-creation of a gold-plated, beveled-glass Buddhist temple (originally built to ward off evil spirits at the Erawan Hotel in Bangkok in the 1950s). Gamblers actually make offerings to this Buddha, who sits outside the main entrance to Caesars; they leave everything from subway tokens to lit candles to piles of mu shu pork on the small patch of marble surrounding the statue. The **Luxor** (tel 702/262–4000, 3900 Las Vegas Blvd. S.) offers its own version of history with King Tut's Tomb, Cleopatra's Needle, and the Hanging Gardens of Babylon gracing the lobby, along with a menacing Sphinx greeting visitors at the entrance. We can't claim that the medieval village at the **Excalibur** (tel 702/597–7777, 3850 Las Vegas Blvd. S.)—replete with jugglers, minstrels, jesters, knights (errant and otherwise), and assorted lords and ladies—is authentic, but it could inspire a lecture on such related topics as chivalry, apprenticeship, and serfdom. The glory years of automobile history are on display at the Imperial Palace's **Antique Auto Collection** (tel 702/731–3311; 3535 Las Vegas Blvd. S.; open 5pm–1am; $6.95 adults, $3 children), with vintage cars like Hitler's 1936 Mercedes-Benz, Mussolini's 1939 Alfa Romeo, Al Capone's 1930 V-16 Cadillac, J.F.K.'s 1962 Lincoln Continental, L.B.J.'s 1964 Caddy, Truman's 1950 Lincoln Cosmopolitan, F.D.R.'s 1936 V-16 Cadillac, and Eisenhower's 1950 Chrysler Imperial, not to mention the truly eccentric '54 Chrysler owned by the notoriously germ-phobic Howard Hughes—the trunk includes an intricate air-purification system.

As for Las Vegas history, head a block off the Strip to the lobby of the **Las Vegas Hilton** (tel 702/732–5111, 3000 Paradise Rd.). Hook a sharp right once you're inside, and you'll come face to face with the King himself—a bronze statue of pre-blubber Elvis Presley, Las Vegas's patron saint. Bugsy Siegel's place in Vegas's history books is commemorated at the **Flamingo Hilton** (tel 702/733–3111, 3555 Las Vegas Blvd. S.) with a small brick memorial and a rose garden (Bugsy once planted American Beauties on the Flamingo's grounds).

Electronic warfare... At the Luxor (tel 702/262–4000, 3900 Las Vegas Blvd. S.), **Sega VirtuaLand** (open until midnight) is an 18,000-square-foot treasure trove of futuristic games developed by Sega Enterprises, the world's leading manufacturer of video games. Sega test-markets all its latest gear here, from stand-up games to cockpit shoot-outs, all of them interactive. Sandwiched between two levels of the pyramid's mezzanine, the arcade leaves something to be desired, decor-wise—it's a dark, eerie environment that, if nothing else, keeps your attention focused on the Daytona race-car simulator, virtual-reality battleground, and 360-degree flight simulator machines. While some of the Strip's other casino hotels, such as Caesars Palace, Circus Circus, Stratosphere, and the Monte Carlo, have arcade areas, none of them comes close to what Sega's testing at the Luxor. At the Excalibur (tel 702/597–7777, 3850 Las Vegas Blvd. S.), **Fantasy Faire** (open until midnight) is a hokey midway-style setup that boasts the usual tired collection of pinball machines and pinging video games, but in keeping with the hotel's theme, it also offers medieval-themed carnival games like the Electronic Crossbow, where kiddies can play Robin Hood. Off the Strip is **Mary K's Arcade** (tel 702/735–3170; 953 E. Sahara Ave.; open 24 hours), in a strip shopping center filled with more Asian restaurants than you can shake a pair of chopsticks at. It's a favorite hangout of Vegas's serious Area 51 and Tetris addicts. The appeal of Mary K's lies entirely in its low prices and all-night hours—certainly not its crusty floors or the geeky-looking teenage crowd drooling onto video screens.

    Virtual World (tel 702/369–3583; 3053 Las Vegas Blvd. S.; open until 11pm weeknights, 1am weekends; $7–$9 per game) is part of an international chain of virtual-reality arcades whose 30-minute games pit combatants from remote locations against each other. You can sit in one of Vegas Virtual World's containment pods at midnight and battle some bleary-eyed cybergeek in San Diego, Chicago, Tokyo, or London—something utterly unimaginable a mere few years ago. Virtual World offers a choice of two scenarios: Battletech or Red Planet. Battletech places its players in suits of armor and sends them to the desert planet Solaris IV for a round of games against other contestants from around the world; Red Planet sends players to the surface of Mars, where they get to race hovercrafts around the canals cut into Mars's surface.

The draw is traditional, mano-a-mano action with an electronic edge at **Ultrazone** (tel 702/734–1577; 2555 S. Maryland Pkwy.; open until 1am; $5 per game), a laser-tag operation that throws players into a darkened, maze-like interior for a futuristic game of capture the flag. Here you're competing against actual living, breathing people (mostly college students from the nearby UNLV campus), which adds a cutthroat element to an otherwise idiotic pastime. Essentially, you strap on a chest pack and run around carrying a laser pistol, hunting down and cyber-killing everything in sight.

Fake nature... If you gotta have spectacle, why not borrow from mother nature, the most spectacular babe of all? Topping the list is the erupting **volcano** outside the South Seas-themed Mirage (tel 702/791–7111, 3400 Las Vegas Blvd. S.), which spews smoke, steam, "lava," and cascades of water every 15 minutes from sunset until midnight. The Mirage has had mixed success with the volcano's realism factor; at times, its recorded sound track has sounded like a herd of elephants who had too many baked beans for dinner, and at other times the volcano's smoke has blown straight into the eyes of the tourists crowding around the attraction (it now stops erupting when there's a stiff breeze—not uncommon in the desert). During the summer of 1996, the volcano was closed down for a few million bucks' worth of enhancements—let's hope they work! Then there are the cascading waterfalls at Circus Circus's **Grand Slam Canyon** and rides at **MGM Grand Adventures** that allow you to plunge into the bowels of another belching volcano or run the Grand Canyon's rapids (for details on both, see "For the kid in all of us," above). Sam's

Town (tel 702/456–7777, 5111 Boulder Hwy.) has re-created a slice of Montana's wilderness in **Town Park** (admission free), a roofed-over expanse of trees, waterfalls, flower
gardens, streams, and mountain vegetation; the air here
actually feels as crisp and cool as on a Rocky Mountain
plateau, a wonderful change from Nevada's desert atmosphere. Then there's the ultra-fake version of nature on display at Caesars Palace's **Omnimax Theater** (tel 702/731–
7110; 3570 Las Vegas Blvd. S.; open Sun–Thur until
10pm, Fri–Sat until 11pm; $7), whose 10-story screen
allows viewers to blast off into space, cruise the Grand
Canyon (for a change), or go on safari in the Serengeti.

Real nature (as real as anything gets in Vegas)...
The pool area at **The Tropicana** (tel 702/739–2222, 3801
Las Vegas Blvd. S.) seems hacked from the luxuriant
undergrowth, a virtual rain forest of carefully "wild" gardens snaking around lagoons and waterfalls. Spanning
this gorgeous pool and garden area is Wildlife Walk,
inhabited by dozens of chattering, cawing monkeys,
snakes, toucans, cockatoos, parrots, flamingos, peacocks,
swans, cranes, and macaws from across Central and South
America. If you come during feeding time (around 6pm)
you'll be able to pet and feed some of the tamer birds;
some animals are removed at 7pm, but many others stay
visible through the night, and you can view it all for free.
The bird sanctuary behind the **Flamingo Hilton** (tel 702/
733–3111; 3555 Las Vegas Blvd. S.; open 24 hours;
admission free) is home to Vegas's only penguins not making their livings in a production-show routine, as well as
ibis, black swans, cockatoos, and (of course) pink flamingos. The white tiger exhibit at the **Mirage** (tel 702/791–
7111, 3400 Las Vegas Blvd. S.) does double duty as a full-
time home for the trained beasts used onstage in Siegfried
& Roy's long-running production show. Often, one or
more of the tigers is visible (napping, usually) behind the
exhibit's thick plexiglass windows. Adjacent to the
Mirage's tropically lush pool area, you'll find the Dolphin
Habitat, a marine environment displaying dolphins res-
cued from unsuitable conditions at nickel-and-dime water
parks around the country. Free Willy indeed.

Hollywood East... Before leaving Las Vegas, cinemaphiles
might get a kick out of Debbie Reynolds's shrine to movie

HANGING OUT ⟋ THE LOWDOWN

making, called, appropriately enough, the **Hollywood Movie Museum** (tel 702/734–0711; 305 Convention Center Dr.; open until 11pm; $7.95), which houses her collection of memorabilia. Displays range from whatever the MGM Grand couldn't finesse from the *Wizard of Oz* set, to costumes like Marilyn Monroe's famed "subway" dress from *The Seven Year Itch*, and La Liz's grand-entrance-to-Rome duds from *Cleopatra*. And to see how the stars motored in style, check out the **Imperial Palace Antique Auto Collection** (tel 702/731–3311; 3535 Las Vegas Blvd. S.; open 5pm–1am; $6.95 adults, $3 children), which features classics like Jimmy Cagney's 1937 Duesenberg (and around three dozen other Duzys), Liberace's eggshell-colored 1981 Zimmer Golden Spirit, and W.C. Fields's 1938 Cadillac touring car (the full bar in the back seat will come as no surprise).

Going to the chapel... Somewhere in the neighborhood of 1.3 million people live in Clark County, yet the county clerk issues more than 100,000 marriage licenses each year. This city's marriage industry is big, big business; you can get a wedding ring slipped onto your finger in dozens of places both on and off the Strip, 24 hours a day. Before the ceremony, you gotta swing past the city's **Office of the Civil Marriage Commissioner** (no calls, 309 S. 3rd St.) or over to the county's **Marriage License Bureau** (tel 702/455–3156, 200 S. 3rd St.) a block away, to grab a $35 marriage license; both are open Monday through Thursday until midnight, round the clock Friday through Sunday. You don't need a blood test, you don't need to suffer through a session with a marriage counselor, you don't even need to have a ring, though most of the wedding chapels located outside of casino hotels have gift shops where you can max out your plastic with anything from a gardenia to a garter. A wedding chapel ceremony's going to set you back around $100, with everything you touch costing that much more (as in bouquet, limo, photo, and a tux or gown). Atmospheres range from fantasy factories like the **Little White Chapel** (tel 702/382–5943, 1301 Las Vegas Blvd. S.), which even has a drive-in window, or the **Little Church of the West** (tel 702/739–7971, 3960 Las Vegas Blvd. S.), to the 100-story Heavenly Garden, Renaissance Court, or Cupid's Terrace wedding chapels inside the **Stratosphere**'s tower (tel 702/380–

7777, 2000 Las Vegas Blvd. S.), with all of Vegas spread out beneath you. At Excalibur's **Canterbury Chapel** (tel 702/597–7777, 3850 Las Vegas Blvd. S.), the hotel can supply you with a justice of the peace in a King Arthur get-up. The **Rio** (tel 702/252–7777, 3700 W. Flamingo Rd.) has two wedding chapels, where you can take the plunge in Copacabana style. If you really want to go all out, The Little White Chapel will even arrange a heli-copter ceremony—you can get married while choppering up and down the length of the Strip, or even hovering over Lake Mead. (The parachuting Elvis impersonators you'll have to arrange on your own.)

You can watch for free; stand outside the wedding chapel in any hotel to see the starry-eyed processions. You can also politely ask to sit in a pew and watch the cere-mony. You're likely to be the only one there, and it can be one of the screwiest, saddest, most joyful experiences of your life. But if you're thinking of getting hitched, book reservations way, way ahead in order to walk down the aisle on a holiday or a weekend. With more than 200,000 brides and grooms clogging the city's marriage mills each year, vow-happy gridlock isn't a joke, especially when cou-ples are lined up like Chevys heading into a car wash.

A cup of joe and some art to go... Sometimes, in the middle of this city's drink/gamble/party atmosphere, the soul needs a strong jolt of caffeine delivered in the quiet environment of a coffee bar. Even if you don't go to AA meetings, these are still great places to hang—they tend to be frequented by locals, and at some spots you may even find yourself slipping into a meaningful conversation (hint: don't lead off with a line about how much you won gambling). What's more, just about every decent Vegas coffeehouse does double-duty as an art gallery, drawing local artists as well as off-duty dancers and performers to these cozy haunts. **Jazzed Cafe & Vinoteca** (tel 702/798–5995; 2055 E. Tropicana Ave.; open until 3am), an East-side joint just a few minutes' drive from the Strip, sports locally created art on its purple walls, plays some terrific jazz CDs—and serves up a mean latte, not to mention Italian appetizers. The city's all-night coffee bar is **Cyber City Cafe** (tel 702/732–2001, 3945 S. Maryland Pkwy.), a hangout for Net surfers and a great place to stop if you're visiting town sans laptop and want to check your e-mail.

Cyber City's forte is definitely not cappuccino, but rather the rotating art exhibits, cushy couches, bulletin boards, and UNLV-meets-the-real-world crowd… at 4am, naturally. Another worthy spot near UNLV is **Cafe Copioh** (tel 702/739–0305; 4550 S. Maryland Pkwy.; open until 2am), a place perked up with a hippie-ish atmosphere— couches, chess boards, tattered paperbacks, and racks piled with every free publication printed in Las Vegas. The artwork on display here is created by the university's art department faculty as well professional artists in need of more wall space. But my personal favorite just may be downtown at the **Enigma Garden Cafe** (tel 702/386– 0999; 918 S. 4th St.; open until 2am), which does triple duty as a coffeehouse, natural foods restaurant, and art gallery. Enigma's outdoor cafe is a shaded refuge of hip sanity from the wild Vegas world—mist is sprayed into the air to keep it cool and fresh—and its exhibition space shows fresh, hard-hitting, and unapologetic artworks. For anyone with an art-collecting bug, Enigma's gallery is a must-see. Most of the artists are involved in **Las Vegas Contemporary Arts Collective**, which also operates an exhibition space two blocks away (tel 702/382–3886, 304 E. Charleston Blvd.), but the hours at this artist-run venture are, at best, unpredictable.

Though not precisely a coffeehouse, **The Attic** (tel 702/388–4088; 1018 South Main St.; open until 10pm, closed Sun) does have an espresso bar and cafe to keep you happy while wading through dozens of racks of vintage clothes, formerly worn by everyone from ranch hands to showgirls—souvenirs of Las Vegas's past.

CD neighborhoods… The **WOW Multimedia Superstore** (tel 702/364–2500, 4580 W. Sahara Ave.) packs music lovers into a cavernous setting seven nights a week until midnight. "WOW" aptly describes the vast selection of CDs (and music aficionados, from long-haired classical buffs to buzz-cut grungers). And if it's 4am, and you've just gotta play the latest Burning Spear to impress that new friend you've met at the Shark, **Odyssey Records** (tel 702/384–4040, 1600 Las Vegas Blvd. S.) is open 24 hours, selling a superb selection of new and alternative music; it's right next door to the White Cross Pharmacy (one of the Strip's landmarks and a great place to buy condoms at 3am—just in case).

Art outside the coffeehouses... Las Vegas does have the modern, well-funded, and starkly configured **Nevada Institute for Contemporary Art** (tel 702/434–2666; 3455 E. Flamingo Rd.), also known as NICA, pronounced "nye-kah." The catch? It has no permanent collection, being only a host for rotating guest exhibitions. But the NICA space (around 3,000 square feet) has a high-ceilinged, broad-walled design that shows off art well; national touring shows stop here, and artists from across the West partici-pate in NICA's invitational exhibitions and compete for the facility's two or three annual one-artist shows. The NICA, open until 8pm on Thursdays, is located in The Cannery, a stunning structure that also houses Wild Oats Market, the city's top natural foods store and vegetarian cafe.

What art sales do take place around here tend to be concentrated in tourist-oriented shopping malls and arcades. Since these galleries cater to high rollers looking to burn a wad or two of newly won cash, don't expect to find bargains, but the work exhibited is generally high-caliber. **Crockett Gallery** (tel 702/253–6336; 2800 W. Sahara Ave.; open until 6pm, closed Sun) is the city's best off-Strip commercial gallery, exhibiting sophisticated landscapes and bronze sculpture. The work shown inside **Galerie Lassen** (tel 702/731–6900; 3500 Las Vegas Blvd. S.; open until 11pm) at Caesars Palace's Forum Shops is certainly the most diverse, international, and exorbitantly priced, ranging from minor 17th-century Flemish oils to regional watercolors; there's also a large group of bronze sculptures, some very nice art glass, and mixed-media paper constructions that are partly based on body castings. The very surprising **P.S. Galleries** (tel 702/733–0705; 3645 Las Vegas Blvd. S.; open until 11pm) inside Bally's Casino Hotel exhibits sculpture, original paintings, and limited-edition prints by established Southwestern artists such as Dale Terbush. The most commendable effort to support Las Vegas artists is at the **Rio Suites** (tel 702/ 252–7777, 3700 W. Flamingo Rd.), which is determined-ly building its own permanent collection of locally creat-ed art. When you visit the Rio, ask at the concierge desk for the self-guided tour brochure, and wander around the hotel admiring the art on display.

Where to blow your winnings... It's remotely possible that you'll walk out of a casino with more cash than you

HANGING OUT ◟ THE LOWDOWN

had when you walked in, though the odds certainly aren't working in your favor (just who do you think pays the mortgages on Vegas's casino hotels, anyway?). If Lady Luck sidles up to you at the slots or blackjack tables, there are lots of places around town where money—especially newly won money—walks and talks. One place you won't want to miss is the recently expanded **Forum Shops** (tel 702/893–4800; 3500 Las Vegas Blvd. S.; open Sun–Thur 10am–11pm, Fri–Sat 10am–midnight) inside Caesars Palace, which has the best late shopping in town. You'll see old geezers escorting bejeweled babes young enough to be their granddaughters, ladies from Midwestern church groups gawking at price tags, rich Japanese folks laboring over their purchasing decisions, and couples who've just won a year's salary at Caesars's craps tables. The roster of shops here includes many well-known names—Bulgari Jewelers, Gucci, North Beach Leathers, the Warner Brothers Studio Store, and Gianni Versace's boutique (Mike Tyson has Versace sealed off from the public whenever he's on one of his Forum Shops spending sprees). And if you ever wanted to dress like a "Vegas pro" (a k a high-priced whore), the Forum Shops have everything from a Victoria's Secret to a leather shop selling knee-high pirate boots. This eye-popping display of conspicuous consumption lines streets that evoke ancient Rome, while the statues of Bacchus and his court of Roman gods "come to life" every hour amid a laser-light display. A real trip.

Just a short walk from the Forum Shops is the **Fashion Show Mall** (tel 702/369–8382, 3200 Las Vegas Blvd. S., open until 9pm), which has several high-end chains such as Neiman Marcus, Saks Fifth Avenue, Bally of Switzerland, and Louis Vuitton. There's a wider range of stores in the **Star Lane** shopping mall at MGM Grand (tel 702/891–1111; 3799 Las Vegas Blvd S.; open 8:30am–midnight), catering primarily to kids and families, as do the new shops inside the second-level mall area at the **Stratosphere** (tel 702/380–7777; 2000 Las Vegas Blvd. S.; open until 11pm). The recently overhauled **Avenue Shops** at Bally's (tel 702/739–4111; 3645 Las Vegas Blvd. S.; open until 11am) now include an art gallery, several fancy clothing and sporting-gear stores, a wedding chapel, and a sushi bar. At Excalibur's **Medieval Village** (tel 702/597–7777, 3850 Las Vegas

Blvd. S., open until 11pm), the stores range from kitschy boutiques to an apothecary selling lots of new-age talismans; there's even a place that sells handmade knights' swords (the real deal), imported from Spain and sharpened to a perfect edge, in case you need some last-minute equipment for a duel.

If outlet shopping is more your speed—maybe the slots just gobbled up all your cash—you can find discounts on everything from appliances to appliquéd evening wear at **Las Vegas Factory Stores** (tel 702/897–9090; 9155 Las Vegas Blvd. S.; open until 8pm), with notable names including Geoffrey Beene, Mikasa, and American Tourister (to lug home your purchases); and at **Belz Factory Outlet World** (tel 702/897–7271; I-15 at the Blue Diamond Exchange; open until 9pm), where casualwear reigns supreme—look for labels like Bass, Danskin, Nike, and Levi.

A little something to remember Vegas by... If you're a connoisseur of the deliciously tacky, Vegas may actually disappoint (well, aside from those Liberace candelabra Christmas tree ornaments or Elvis lamps). Yes, there are plenty of cheesy shops that print "Las Vegas" on everything from T-shirts to silver spoons; dozens of souvenir shops crowd along Fremont Street and the Strip's Las Vegas Boulevard. Some of these stores are so absurdly tasteless you'll break out in laughter the minute you walk through their doors: Who could have imagined an entire wall devoted to myriad styles of stuffed Elvis and Wayne Newton dolls? Dice clocks are memorably awful: they're made of colored plastic, with dice rather than numerals circling the face. You'll find a fine assortment of dice clocks (as well as decent Indian jewelry and T-shirts) on the Strip at **Fabulous Gifts** (tel 702/732–2107; 3025 Las Vegas Blvd. S.; open 24 hours) and downtown at **Las Vegas Western Village** (tel 702/386–6933; 323 Fremont St.; open until midnight).

The **Hard Rock Hotel** (tel 702/693–5000; 4455 Paradise Rd.; open until midnight) didn't set out to make souvenirs when it designed its casino chips, but check em out—the $25 chips are printed with an image of Jimi Hendrix, and $100 chips have Tom Petty's ditty "You Got Lucky, Babe" emblazoned on their backs. So many people have been walking off with the Hard Rock's chips that this unexpected influx of cash has become a trackable source of casino income (the chips cost Hard Rock about 50 cents apiece to manufacture; multiply that by $25 or $100…). Similarly, the kitschy booze containers served up at various venues have become must-have souvenirs, thanks to alcohol-friendly local laws that allow folks to walk along the Strip and downtown sidewalks with wine coolers, bottles of beer, and margaritas (shades of Bourbon Street). For sheer tackiness, few vessels beat the tapered, plastic piña colada glasses from the **Enter the Night** production show at the Stardust (tel 702/732–6111, 3000 Las Vegas Blvd. S.), or the skull-shaped glasses from the **Battle Bar** at Treasure Island (tel 702/894–7111, 3300 Las Vegas Blvd. S.). The drinks cost around $10, but you not only get to keep the glass, you can also snag a bird's-eye seat for Treasure Island's nightly Pirates-versus-Brits spectacle while sipping whatever concoction shivers your timbers, matey.

Where to get a cut and a blow-dry job... A Little Off the Top (tel 702/258–5411; 5720 W. Charleston Blvd.; open until 7pm, closed Sun) is a little over the top: A curvaceous, lingerie-clad lady will shampoo, cut, fluff, even color your hair for $25–$50. This is one of those "only in Vegas" experiences, but keep in mind that these women are stylists, nothing more: Be on your best behavior or else they'll trim more than your locks.

Tattoo you... Here in the City that Never Blinks, you too can join the hordes of tattooed trendoids who will one day be shelling out zillions of dollars to have blue- and red-dyed patterns removed from beneath their skin by powerful lasers. **Tattoos R Us** (tel 702/387–6969, 320 E. Charleston Blvd.) is the city's largest and most popular tattoo parlor, staying open seven nights a week—until midnight on weekends, and 10pm the rest of the time. You can even have your whatever or whatchamacallit pierced here in just a few minutes. **Desert Heat Tattoos** (tel 702/383–6600; 2140 W. Charleston Blvd.; open Mon–Thur until 11pm, Fri–Sun until 1am, closed Sun) is a more serious sort of tattoo parlor, the kind of place where you're likelier to run into a biker having his calf redone than a college kid squirming over his first-ever arm tattoo.

Vibrator city... Vegas has lots of shops selling sex toys and fantasy gear; the largest and most popular are **Rancho Adult Entertainment** (tel 702/645–6106; 4820 N. Rancho Dr.; open until 10pm) and, close to the Strip, **Tropicana Adult Superstore** (tel 702/798–0144; 3850 W. Tropicana Ave.; open until midnight). Tropicana Adult Superstore is set up more like a supermarket than anything having to do with something naughty; Rancho Adult Entertainment is run by a group of grandmotherly types who have no problem looking you squarely in the eyes while counseling you on the purchase of a variable-speed vibrator. Anyone into the leather scene will definitely want to check out the handcuffs, whips, and Nazi-bikers-on-holiday gear at **Lock, Stock & Leather** (tel 702/796–9801, 4640 Paradise Rd., open Sun–Thur until 10pm, Fri–Sat until 2am; closed Mon). Drag queens in last-minute need of a push-up bra or size-12 high heels can rely upon the **Cat O' Nine Tails Boutique** (tel 702/258–9754; 1717 S. Decatur Blvd.; open until 10pm).

Forbidden fruit... It may seem hypocritical of the world's T&A capital, but prostitution is outlawed in Clark County, which includes all of Las Vegas. The state of Nevada does, however, permit prostitution on a county-by-county basis, and the closest place offering legal sex for sale is an hour away from Las Vegas: Nye County, especially the cathouse capital, Pahrump (even sounds like the punchline of an off-color joke, doesn't it?). Places like the **Chicken Ranch** (tel 702/382–7870; Homestead Rd., Pahrump), the **Cherry Patch Ranch** (tel 702/372–5251; Hwy. 160, Pahrump), and others will, ahem, service clients' every need, right down to arranging for a shuttle van to pick up and return them to their hotels. Still, you have to be crazy to do this sort of thing in the age of AIDS. Don't say we didn't warn you.

late nigh

t dining

Cheap food isn't just a
concept in this city, it's a
religion. And talk about
all-you-can-eat—Las Vegas
is the promised land for the
kind of chowhounds who
like to gorge themselves,

consuming enough food at one meal to sustain a small munic-ipality. If you think that doesn't sound like a very promising recipe for culinary excellence, well, for the most part it hasn't been. When I first started visiting Las Vegas in the late 1980s, finding anything other than a fairly standard dining experi-ence was nearly impossible. While there were some decent Italian, Chinese, and Mexican places scattered around the city, basically Vegas was a dining disappointment. But fast-forward to the second half of the 1990s, and the situation's done a 180-degree turnaround. Yeah, there are still tons of restaurants inside the casino hotels that are content to dish up fabulous prime ribs (they're *always* done that well), incredibly rich and gooey eggs benedict, and towering BLTs. But with Vegas now one of the nation's fastest-growing metropolitan areas, attract-ing tens of thousands of habitual restaurant-goers from other urban areas, restaurant developers and owners have begun to open up new places from one end of the city to the other. Add to this a fresh generation of expense-account conventioneers, and you've got the sort of customer base that can support a sophisticated new breed of restaurants. Many casino hotels have opened their doors to either celebrity chefs or sophisti-cated restauranteurs with proven track records, who have developed successful places in cities such as San Francisco, Chicago, and New York. Even a smallish version of a star chef's restaurant can do 500 high-priced dinners on an average night, which makes it all very worthwhile. Mark Miller—the Santa Fe chef whose Coyote Cafe is credited with lifting Southwestern cuisine out of its Tex-Mex doldrums—has a Coyote Cafe inside the MGM Grand. Right around the cor-ner is the restaurant of New Orleans's nouveau-seafood mas-ter, Emiril Lagasse, a legendary chef from Commander's Palace whose fabulous place on Tchoupitoulas Street is a food-ies' mecca. And ever since Wolfgang Puck opened the doors of his Spago inside Caesars Palace's Forum Shops, ordinary folks like Danny DeVito and Joan Rivers have a new favorite place to hang out whenever they're in town, munching goat-cheese pizza with grilled portobellos and roasted garlic. Along with all this, in the past few years Las Vegas has been invaded by corporate-backed theme restaurants, where the emphasis is as much on merchandising logowear and tie-in paraphernalia as it is on the quality of the kitchen. Aimed squarely at middle-American and foreign tourists, these theme restaurants have caught on like wildfire. As this book goes to press, nearly a dozen more are planned at various locations along the Strip, joining the half dozen already packing 'em in like cattle.

A Word About Prices

Historically, the casino hotels used gambling revenues to sub-sidize restaurant prices, which is how Vegas first became known as the home of incredible food deals—your legendary dollar breakfasts, three-buck steak dinners, and six-buck surf-'n'-turf feasts. Be sure to check the two-for-one and discount specials printed up in *What's On, Showbiz,* and *Today in Las Vegas.* But be warned: Many of these places offer those deals only at certain hours, meaning that if you want to cash in, you've got to deal with lines and some elbow-to-elbow seating arrangements. This isn't to say that only cheap dining experi-ences fly in Las Vegas. Many casino hotels also have what are referred to as "gourmet rooms"—high-end restaurants whose chief purpose is to pamper high rollers. Prices are kept high enough so that comped customers will feel that they're being given a real treat, but as fine dining goes, the prices here are still fairly reasonable. To make a restaurant concept pay its own way in Vegas's competitive climate, economies of scale dictate serving several hundreds of diners at once—many restaurants along the Strip and downtown tend to be large and crammed wall to wall with diners during peak hours. But with the advent of the new breed of upscale restaurants, the tide has turned somewhat. These chi-chi newcomers go for a much smaller number of tables—you just can't attract a high-paying crowd with a feed-trough atmosphere. If they're successful, though, there's such a crush to get inside, nobody blinks at the prices or complains about waiting a while to be seated.

When To Eat

The city's better restaurants generally close at 10pm on week-nights and midnight on weekends, though there are many good places that keep their doors open until 2am. After that, you're pretty much limited to the 24-hour cafes and restau-rants inside the casino hotels, as well as the usual sort of all-night breakfast places and burger joints that are fixtures on America's nightscape. If that sounds like dismal news, realize that at most of these casino hotel cafes there's damn good food served at a fraction of what it would normally cost, and often these all-night hang-out scenes throw in great people-watching along with your waffles and java. To avoid being part of the whirlwind action in a packed and frantic restau-rant, simply walk through the door after 9pm, keeping in mind that on peak-season weekends and during large con-ventions, you'll almost always need a reservation right up until 10pm.

Late Night Dining Near The Strip and Paradise Road

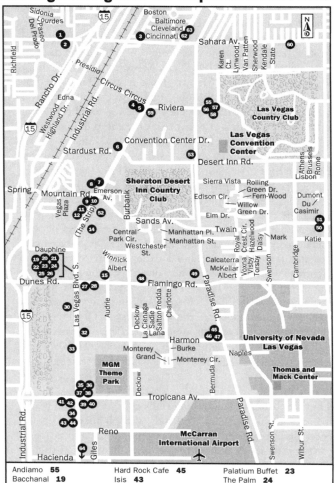

Andiamo **55**
Bacchanal **19**
Battista's Pizza Rio **15**
Benihana **56**
Bertolini's **20**
Bistro Le Montrachet **57**
Camelot **41**
Circus Circus Buffet **4**
Country Star **30**
Coyote Cafe **37**
Dive **8**
Dragon Noodle Company **33**
El Gaucho **39**
Emeril's **36**
Fog City Diner **49**
Gatsby's **35**
Golden Steer **3**
Guadalajara Grille **2**
Hamada of Japan **48**

Hard Rock Cafe **45**
Isis **43**
Kabuki Japanese
    Restaurant **51**
Kady's **64**
Komol Thai **60**
Las Olas **28**
Lookout Cafe **10**
Magical Empire **21**
Margaritagrille **58**
Market Place Buffet **32**
Ming Terrace **14**
Mizuno's Teppan Dining **40**
Moongate/Mikado **12**
Morton's of Chicago **7**
Mortoni's **46**
Mr. Lucky's 24/7 **47**
Oz Buffet **38**
Palace Court **22**

Palatium Buffet **23**
The Palm **24**
Papyrus **44**
Planet Hollywood **25**
Primavera **34**
Ristorante Italiano **59**
Ristorante Riva **11**
Romano's Macaroni Grill **1**
Rosewood Grille **52**
Seasons **27**
Sir Galahad's **42**
Sisters Cafe & Grille **62**
Spago **26**
The Steak House **5**
Togoshi Ramen **50**
Top of the World **63**
Treasure Island Buffet **9**
Tres Lobos **6**
Yolle's Brazilian Steakhouse **53**

Las Vegas Area Late Night Dining

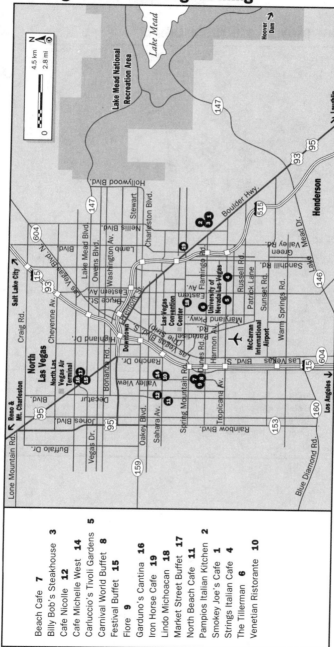

Beach Cafe **7**
Billy Bob's Steakhouse **3**
Cafe Nicolle **12**
Cafe Michelle West **14**
Carluccio's Tivoli Gardens **5**
Carnival World Buffet **8**
Festival Buffet **15**
Fiore **9**
Garduno's Cantina **16**
Iron Horse Cafe **19**
Lindo Michoacan **18**
Market Street Buffet **17**
North Beach Cafe **11**
Pampios Italian Kitchen **2**
Smokey Joe's Cafe **1**
Strings Italian Cafe **4**
The Tillerman **6**
Venetian Ristorante **10**

Downtown Late Night Dining

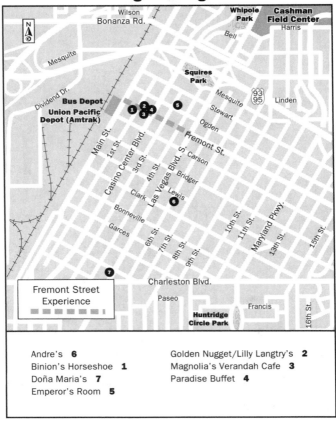

Andre's **6**

Binion's Horseshoe **1**

Doña Maria's **7**

Emperor's Room **5**

Golden Nugget/Lilly Langtry's **2**

Magnolia's Verandah Cafe **3**

Paradise Buffet **4**

The Lowdown

Paradise for pig-outs... Here in Las Vegas there's a traditional form of dining known as the buffet—basically, a pay-one-price sort of cafeteria where the big attraction is the all-you-can-eat concept. Nearly every casino hotel has a buffet room, some fancier than others, some pricier than others, and some serving better food than others. The cheapest buffets run in the range of $3.99 to $5.99—a pretty incredible price considering the amounts of food you can pack away. Within this price category, the various hotel buffets are remarkable consistent; visitors choose among them primarily on the basis of ambience or location. All offer similar food—basically, whatever can be left to sit out for three or four hours without getting either congealed or too dried out. Preparations are geared to a middle-American palate, avoiding spicy sauces or exotic combinations of ingredients. But the cuts of meat are surprisingly decent, the vegetables and fruits fresh, and the desserts appetizing. Breakfast buffets are laid out from about 7am to 10:30 or so; then all the waffles and danish and bacon and eggs are picked up and the lunchtime buffets are hauled out, from about 11am to 2 in the afternoon. Dinner spreads appear starting around 4pm and aren't cleared away until 10 in the evening. Although you can always order off the à la carte menu as well, if the buffet's what you're after, you pay as you enter the room, then grab a plate and start piling it high. At peak dining hours there's always a line to get in, for the simple reason that everyone likes a great deal. And, it goes without saying, any place that promotes itself as having unlimited amounts of nearly free food is bound to attract hordes of foodaholics. The mecca of all cheap buffet meccas is the **Circus Circus Buffet**, that pink-and-white palace of kids' mayhem smack in the middle of the Strip. Walk past the long line of salivating people waiting to be admitted into this buffet room and you'll see more than a few folks who appear to have made numerous return trips to the food-laden tables. You'll also see lots of church groups, penny-pinching conventioneers, families with too many kids, and bewildered Japanese tourists desperate for a taste of America at its weirdest. Definitely see this sideshow while you're in town, keeping in mind that on an average day, Circus Circus will feed thousands (its record day saw more than 17,000 pass through the buffet line—a circus indeed). At the Fremont's **Paradise Buffet**, downtown, the one exception to the general chow-down atmosphere is Friday night, when a well-dressed crowd shows up for the long-standing Seafood Buffet night, offering mounds of Alaskan king crab legs. Strip-wise, Aladdin's **Market Place Buffet** is one of the top deals, a buffet spread loaded with everything from rare prime rib to key lime pies the size of pizzas. When Las Vegas locals go for a buffet, though, they prefer staying off the Strip at places like the **Gold Coast**, which throws in a free drink with dinner and has a friendly wait staff that doesn't keep looking over your shoulder just in case a high roller walks through the door.

A little farther up the food chain... Even Vegas's more expensive buffets keep their prices under $10 for dinner, yet those few bucks make quite a difference—they allow the casino hotels to offer goodies like crab legs, clams casino, fresh raspberries, and pasta made to order. Two of the city's most refreshingly different buffets are in north Las Vegas: the Wednesday seafood feast at the Fiesta's **Festival Buffet** (featuring a gourmet coffee bar) and the awesome fajita stand across the street from the Fiesta at Texas Station's **Market Street Buffet** (which also has decent barbecue). Downtown, **Binion's Horse-shoe** serves a top-notch seafood buffet on Fridays, as well as beef raised on the Binion family's own ranch in Montana. Old-time Vegas atmosphere is Binion's forte. The best buffet in Vegas, though, is just a few blocks west of the Strip at the Rio's **Carnival World Buffet**, where—in true *carioca* spirit—the wait staff comes dressed in next to nothing. Long lines are part of the deal, but you also get ultra-fresh food and a welcome ethnic diversity, thanks to the Brazilian, Chinese, Mexican, and Italian food stations. Members of the casino's slot club pass through a much shorter line, which is a good enough reason to join up the moment you samba through the Rio's doors. MGM Grand's lavish **Oz Buffet** provides welcome variety with its rotating nightly international themes. Caesars Palace's **Palatium Buffet**, which has more of an Italian accent, also has among the Strip's highest buffet prices ($11.95), but the heaping pasta bar and towers of tiramisu and other rich desserts, all commendably executed, make it a real value for the money. Finally, three dining themes (Asian, Italian, and American), middle-level prices, and a free naval battle show staged out in front, every 90 minutes (see Hanging Out) make the **Treasure Island Buffet** a "special night out" candidate for families visiting Vegas on a tight budget.

Only in Vegas... Caesars Palace is the ultimate Las Vegas experience; everything done at Caesars is done with attention to detail, and done extravagantly. **Bacchanal**, the fixed-price feast served by robed gods and goddesses in a bizarre Roman holiday set in 200 AD, is just one example of how far this operation is willing to push a concept. Campy as the experience can be, the food is seriously good; the chefs are urged to be totally creative, going in for exotic ingredients and inventive combinations, and they arrange food flawlessly on the plate. The other example is the **Magical Empire**, a dinner experience that combines Hollywood-esque, magic-themed adventure with standard showroom magic entertainment. To enter the Magical Empire, you're transported via a room-sized elevator down into an underworld maze; one area is designed like a catacomb, another like a performing-arts theater, and yet another like a satanic version of the Vatican. Before and after eating, you're kept moving from site to site, and everywhere you're led, you encounter some sort of illusion, card trick, sleight of hand, or just smoke and mirrors. It definitely distorts your sense of reality— and distracts you from the fact that you're being fed some fairly standard grub for dinner. Different professional magicians are booked in and out of the Magical Empire's theater room to keep the acts fresh, and, in typical Caesars fashion, the staff's dressed in outrageous costumes. It's expensive, but a good show if you've got an extra evening to kill. At the Luxor, the wild dining experience is called

LATE NIGHT DINING ⟨ THE LOWDOWN

Isis, an expensive restaurant decorated to look like the interior of a pharaoh's tomb; the staff dresses in outfits that recall Steve Martin's getup in his "Saturday Night Live" days (remember "King Tut, funky Tut?"). I'm not sure if the pharaohs ate food cooked on hot rocks, but Isis has taken up this unusual twist in culinary presentation, and pulls it off with flair. The food's great, and the service even better, as long as you measure up to the maitre d's jacket-and-tie dress code. For a much lower priced jolt of fantasy, head for the castle-themed Excalibur, where the waiters at **Sir Galahad's** are dressed up like Robin Hoods on prom night. Operating on the assumption that medieval lords and ladies were major meat-eaters, Sir Galahad's pushes the tableside-carved prime rib and Yorkshire pudding for all it's worth. We're not talking fine dining here, but this surprisingly quiet restaurant—a clubby, wood-paneled room decorated with coats of arms and suits of armor—offers a sense of relief from the mayhem that generally reigns throughout the Excalibur.

Let's make a deal... Say it's 2am, you've already cruised a few clubs, and you're suddenly struck by an urge for a shrimp cocktail (come on, it's Vegas... play along). You head downtown and start checking out the marquees hanging over casino hotel entrances and, lo and behold, you've struck it rich! From one end of Fremont Street to the other, these places are practically givin' it away. Swing into the **Golden Nugget**, pass the very hip international beer bar (and the rest of the casino), and head straight to the cafe for your 99-cent shrimp cocktail. Over at **Binion's Horseshoe**, a fabulous throwback to the Las Vegas of yesterday, you snag your 99-cent shrimps in the self-service line of the sandwich bar. Pay an extra nickel for a lemon slice, grab a $2 draft from New Zealand from the superb international beer bar, and find a seat at one of the 30 or so small tables clustered around the piano bar. You can also pull off this routine at other downtown joints like Lady Luck and the Fremont, stuffing so many thumbnail-size shrimp down your throat you'll risk sprouting a dorsal fin. Then there are the steak dinner deals, which deliver some pretty good red meat for the money. Binion's Horseshoe offers the city's best steak-dinner deal, a $3 sirloin that's served with a baked potato and salad from 10pm till 5:45am, but lately the Rio's

Beach Cafe has been nipping at its heels with its 11pm-to-7am deal—a T-bone steak, eggs, and pancakes for just $2.99. If you're in a prime rib kinda mood, run down to the Excalibur's **Sir Galahad's** where, for less than $10, you get a huge slab o' beef as well as the salad bar, a spud, and dessert. Cheap breakfasts are everywhere in Las Vegas, but I'm a dedicated fan of the $2.99 ham-and-eggs deal at the **Gold Coast**, which is served all night and features a platter-size slab of baked ham, on top of which are piled eggs, hash browns, and toast—a fine way to cap off an evening of Vegas mayhem.

After midnight... By far the coolest place in Vegas to hang out after midnight is the Hard Rock's **Mr. Lucky's 24/7**, a bastion of Vegas's over-30 chic set, and home to dynamite food tempered with a distinctive Southwestern flair—grilled seafood steaks, towering chicken salads, huge slices of apple pie, and ice-cream sundaes. The atmosphere doesn't strive to re-create the feeling of a Honolulu Denny's—the unfortunate decor choice for many of Vegas's all-night joints. Instead, Mr. Lucky's has a hip take on the roadhouse look, with battered highway signs and leather booths combined with brushed-aluminum tables and a bleached wood counter from which you can watch the chefs cook. Mr. Lucky's is where band members hang out after finishing their concerts, where models stretch their luscious legs or flex their solid pecs after a hard night on a dance floor, and where a younger, moneyed set takes up residence in some of the larger booths from around 2am until dawn. If you can't make it down to the Hard Rock, the best alternative is the Rio's **Beach Cafe**, where the 24-hour crowd tends more toward off-work dancers and dyed-in-the-wool club-crawlers hanging out at the nearby Club Rio. The bill of fare deals in burgers, seafood salads, and the like, and there are some super late-night meal deals. The cluttered, overdone design theme is more reminiscent of Miami's South Beach than of South America, but hey, it's late—at least the decor will keep you awake. While most of the Strip's and downtown's casino hotels have all-night cafes, some are better than others, not just for the food—the menu is pretty standard everywhere, with burgers, ham and eggs, and pancakes—but for great people-watching. Downtown, the cafe at **Binion's Horseshoe** is the sort of place where men wear bolos and the ladies all seem to be chain-smoking Newports; if you can get past the smoky atmosphere, the food's great. Another good bet downtown is **Magnolia's Verandah** cafe, a 24-hour joint at the Four Queens, where the food's cheap and served all night; it's an especially fun place to hang out and meet the natives after the casino's Monday Night Jazz bash wraps up. On the Strip, the Stratosphere's pleasant **Sisters Cafe & Grille** has a Cajun flair to its cooking; the Strat's lounge band keeps crankin' until 2, 3, or 4am (depending on which night of the week you're there). I also like Treasure Island's **Lookout Cafe** for its huge sandwiches, as well as for the view of lagoons and warships out in front, though the battling sea pirates give up the ship after 11:30pm. Locals in need of a late-night food fix have a soft spot in their hearts for the cafes inside casino hotels operated by the Stations company; they employ friendly staffs and are easy to get into because they're off the Strip. Near the Strip, there's Palace Station's **Iron Horse Cafe**, a fave for Vegas working folks who just want good, cheap standards like burgers, steak and eggs, tuna sandwiches, and the like at a crazy hour. Its sister spot is down on Boulder Strip—Boulder Station's Iron Horse Cafe. The surprisingly nice **Smokey Joe's Cafe** at Sam's Town is another off-Strip hang for locals. Joe's ain't Smokey because the nicotine-addicted crowd comes here (though in this loony town, cigs are still a very big thing), but because of the tasty smoked ribs, barbecued chicken, and an all-you-can-crunch salad bar.

Inv-Asian... Since the late eighties, Las Vegas has become a stop for Asian tour groups doing the usual Disneyland/ Grand Canyon circuit. The city's casino hotel operators have responded by rolling out their culinary welcome mats—practically overnight, nearly half the buffets in town began featuring Chinese, Korean, or Japanese foods. Off the Strip, there's an Asian-restaurant district inside the old shopping center at 953 East Sahara Avenue (a k a Commercial Center). Some of Vegas's most authentic (not to mention cheapest) hotspots are here, cheek-by-jowl with Asian nightclubs, karaoke joints, and even a salsa music nightclub. The best of the lot? Depends on what your tastes are in Asian foods, but I can vouch for the quality of **Komol Thai**, a place where the local Asian population throngs on weekends, and where, if you're really lucky, you'll stumble upon a traditional Thai wedding reception. The pad thai here is predictably wonderful. **Togoshi Ramen**, an authentic Japanese noodle joint just two miles east of the Strip, serves food that's cheap, good, and delicately flavorful. The very wonderful **Hamada of Japan**, a clean and unflaggingly friendly sushi restaurant and sukiyaki house close to the Strip, keeps its chefs working until 2am serving top-quality tuna and tempura rolls, skewers of eel, Vegas rolls (with fried clams), spider rolls (with soft-shell crab), and cold bottles of Sapporo beer. **Kabuki Japanese Restaurant**, another off-Strip sushi joint with a loyal following, falls way short of Hamada on several levels; unfortunately, keeping the place looking spotless is one of them. Downtown's casino hotels have a couple of decent Chinese restaurants, namely the Golden Nugget's upscale **Lilly Langtry's** and Lady Luck's **Emperor's Room** (which still serves clichéd classics like chop suey and egg foo young). But to really get a handle on how far Vegas will go to accommodate Asian tourists, you've got to head down to the Strip. Luxor's **Papyrus** is a real find, especially for its innovative take on Polynesian cuisine, complete with food cooked tableside on 500-degree rocks and a dining room filled with palm trees and waterfalls. Don't miss the fried ice-cream dessert. The tableside cooking at the Las Vegas Hilton's **Benihana** may be an old warhorse of a concept, but in Vegas it's done with an enthusiasm bordering on perfection. There's something mystifyingly hypnotic about watching the Benihana chefs—they flail away with razor-sharp knives and meat cleavers, slicing up your beef, veggies, and shrimp. The typically over-the-top Vegas setting—koi ponds, nature-run-wild sound effects, and a half-dozen stone dragon statues—only helps put one in the proper mood. If you enjoy this culinary showmanship as much as I do, then also check out the Tropicana's **Mizuno's Teppan Dining**, which has a much more casual, jungle-esque setting than rival Benihana's, and keeps its prices lower. The Monte Carlo's **Dragon Noodle Company** scores with good quality and low prices, emphasizing freshly made soups, rotisserie-cooked chicken, and imported teas. (Also check out the casino's brewpub.) The Imperial Palace's **Ming Terrace** cooks great specialties from across the Chinese realm, from Szechuan to Canton, and it's reasonably priced and stays open late. **Mikado** borrows a little bit of everything, from fine dining at regular tables to the teppan-style tableside cooking that wows all the tourists. One of its strongest suits, however, is its setting, which replicates the design of a traditional Japanese home (built to American proportions, that is).

Theme for a day... From the looks of things, the day will soon come when a drive down the Strip will bring you past so many Hollywood-style names and places you'll need a *TV Guide* to find your way around. Starting at the Strip's midpoint, the northernmost of these theme restaurants is the submarine-styled **Dive**, Steven Spielberg's joint, featuring burgers, ribs, and baked chicken. Jutting out of the side of Fashion Show Mall, it looks like the bow of a Soviet submarine trying to torpedo the Treasure Island (now *that* would be a helluva show). Of course, Dive serves submarine sandwiches by the boatload (more than 20 varieties at last count) and has an extensive kids' menu with lots of stuff to keep Junior happy. Vegas's obsession with theme dining has inevitably brought in an outpost of **Planet Hollywood**, a rock 'n' roll memorabilia haven that serves overpriced "California-style" food (crab omelettes with avocado, patty melts, chocolate shakes, etc.) in a pseudo-hipster setting tucked in a corner of the Fourum Shop at Caesars. If you're on the east side of the Strip, duck into that burger joint par excellence, the **Hard Rock Cafe** at the corner of Harmon Street and Paradise Road, right outside the entrance to the Hard Rock Casino Hotel. Don't expect to stumble onto anyone other than tourists, teens, and twentysomethings here, though. (Any star worth his or her drawing power, as well as local trendoids, hang out *inside* the Hard Rock Hotel, at Mr. Lucky's 24/7.) Another into the field is the **Country Star**, a place serving second-rate (and way overpriced) roadhouse fare—chili burgers, pork ribs, and fried chicken. Live appearances by country-music performers help this place hawk burgers, leather jackets, $25 T-shirts, and enough countrified junk to put an Oklahoma flea market to shame. Merchandising is what theme restaurants are all about, which is why Serbian soldiers wear Hard Rock T-shirts and waitpersons at Country Star place merchandise order forms on your table at the same time they bring menus. So why expect the food at these retail operations to be anything exceptional? If this city's dreamers and real-estate developers have their way, in the next few years Vegas will become home to still more packaged schlock: the Harley-Davidson Cafe, the Motown Cafe, the Rain Forest Cafe, House of Blues, Hurricane Harry's, and Billboard Live are all in the air.... I can hardly wait.

Plush and pampered away from the Strip... Off the Strip there are dozens of great places where fine dining is approached with the reverence it deserves; their attention to detail rivals, if not exceeds, what's found in the Strip's casino hotels. **The Tillerman** has been Vegas's favorite seafood place for years. Its interior theme is stolen straight from the pages of a suburban decor magazine, but careful attention to specialties like grilled halibut and Gulf Coast oysters has earned it a stellar reputation. The Tillerman's wonderful wine list is second only to the one at **André's**, a refined French restaurant downtown that attracts a well-heeled crowd of Vegas movers and shakers cutting real-estate deals in the dark dining room. The **Fog City Diner** is worth the effort it may take to get on the busy reservation list. This San Francisco–based operation has turned Vegas on its culinary ear by setting up on its own, away from the Strip, and doing a great business. The Fog City's prices are great, the authentic diner decor is second only to that of the Buckhead Diner in Atlanta, and the kitchen's nouveau-Californian-meets-classic-American innovations leave little wonder why San Francisco is one of the nation's foremost culinary centers. Quiet courtyards in upscale shopping centers seem to work well for a number of the city's better restaurants. **Cafe Nicolle** and **Cafe Michelle West** are two outstanding examples: Serving nouveau/Continental/Euro cuisine, both attract the city's business crowd for lunch and turn up the romance quotient during the dinner hours; both places have piano bars to boot. Cafe Nicolle's crowd tends to be more of a dress-up set, the type of well-heeled folks who treat their pals to bottles of Dom Perignon to celebrate closing a big business deal, while the clientele at Cafe Michelle seems to want less visibility—maybe they're still finalizing their big deals, and who knows who could be listening in? An up-and-coming contender for the title of best yuppie hangout, the **North Beach Cafe** would be a neighborhood-type place if Vegas had any real neighborhoods; as it is, its location on the west side of the city in an upscale strip mall is, at least, far from the Strip's madding crowds. No piano bar here, but an art-filled interior adds a casual touch of class, and the innovative pasta-oriented menu would be right at home in Santa Monica or Scottsdale. If you just can't stay away from the Strip, one of my favorite upscale spots is the **Rosewood Grille**, a refreshing relief from the non-stop scene going on just a few yards away. The Rosewood reminds me of the sort of places my dad, who owned a few restaurants, would take me to on his rounds of favorite spots in Manhattan: dark and sophisticated, with professional waiters, crisp tablecloths, a huge wine list, and a menu built around the tried and true—lobsters, prime rib, scampi, and Caesar salad.

Gourmet rooms... When it comes to taking care of its friends, Vegas can't be beat. From the comped rooms casinos offer high rollers to the free drinks the Gold Coast throws in with its already cheap buffet, this is a city that knows how to pamper its best customers, and one very potent tool for pleasing them is the hotel's "gourmet room," the upscale in-house restaurant. Casino bosses oh-so-generously reward big players with free meals in these plush salons—coincidentally keeping those gamblers on premises, in hopes that they will eventually return to the tables and restore some of their winnings to the casino. Despite a well-deserved reputation for delicious excess—outrageous staff costumes, campy decor, marble sheathing every inch of concrete in the place—Caesars Palace makes a habit of doing things right: You can be assured of good-quality food, service, and amenities anywhere on Caesars's spread. Quality is why its **Bacchanal** is worth its $70 fixed price: Nothing is left to chance, from the wines selected for your dinner to the three-hour, seven-course meal served by waiters built like centurions. Yes, it's dining as theater, and it all may be way over the top, like Dennis Rodman wearing a miniskirt on his Harley. But on the other hand, why the hell not? If you can't do this in Vegas, you can't do it, period. At the more restrained **Palace Court**, also at Caesars Palace (it shares top-notch chefs and kitchen staff with Bacchanal), the culinary focus is on more traditional French and American restaurant fare such as *steak au* *poivre*, broiled lobster, and *cassoulet*. **Gatsby's** at the MGM Grand does as great a job with food (and even a little better on wine) as Bacchanal, but without the costumery—which may be a plus or a minus, depending on your point of view. Gatsby's à la carte specialties at Gatsby's are an inspired blend of nouveau California and classic French cuisine, served in a plush 70-seat dining room where the staff seems to outnumber customers by two to one. The **Seasons** restaurant inside Bally's is a real class act, with perfect service and a low-lit atmosphere that relaxes you the minute you walk through its door. Okay, so the menu features many of the same standards as most other Vegas gourmet rooms; the twist here is that the menu changes according to market availability—no lobster when it's out of season, soft-shell crabs only when they're available from the Chesapeake, and vegetables that are flown in fresh from around the world. **Bistro Le Montrachet** at the Las Vegas Hilton has the sort of deal-making setting that businessmen love, which is why reservations here are next to impossible to get during the larger conventions. Service is straight out of the snobby school of French haute cuisine, and the food is French classic all the way—everything from coq au vin to mousse au chocolat, with a wine list that tops out at 400 selections. Le Montrachet's elegant, upscale bistro decor would put any Parisian immediately at home, and its surprisingly active bar does double duty as one of the favored meeting grounds for Vegas's well-heeled establishment types. When it put together the staff of the Northern Italian gourmet room, **Fiore**, the Rio did things right by bringing aboard French-trained chefs and attentive Italian waiters. Table linens and low lighting set a formal mood, and the food too is solemnly impressive; this place takes itself seriously, right down to the au courant cigar-smoking lounge. The Excalibur's **Camelot** is also very strong on both service and wine list, with a focus on roasted and grilled meats. Stratosphere's **Top of the World** is, as you could guess, inside the 12-story structure atop this casino hotel's 1,149-foot tower; it rotates 360 degrees each hour, which makes this place a shoe-in for the best view in Vegas. The view would no doubt draw visitors anyway, but Top of the World strives to look classy with glossy, modern decor, and serves up respectable renditions of pricey Continental standbys—steaks, lobster, pastas, and flambéed desserts. Three hoity-toity, out-of-town places have recently opened branches inside casino hotels on the Strip. In the MGM Grand, the **Coyote Cafe** is a very upscale Southwestern/nouveau restaurant spawned by chef Mark Miller's Coyote Cafe in Santa Fe. The food's not as spicy as that of the parent restaurant, but otherwise the standards are kept high—this is definitely one of Vegas's best restaurants. The emphasis here is on unusual combinations of fresh ingredients from Mexico—chiles, sauces, and marinades—over grilled seafood, steaks, and tamales. At Caesars Palace, **Spago** is Wolfgang Puck's trend-setting place serving fabulous pizzas and pastas, with an L.A.-style people-watching scene (look!… is that Natalie Cole?). **Emeril's**, also in the MGM Grand, is the brainchild of Emeril Lagasse, a young New Orleans chef who does seafood Cajun-style without drowning everything in butter. He more than deserves his star status for his fabulous touch with healthy ingredients; what's more, Emeril's manages to feel like an island of N'Awlins tranquility in the tossing seas of the MGM's mega-scene.

Carnivoraciousness... Circus Circus has Vegas's best palace of red-meat worship in **The Steak House**, a dark and quiet restaurant dedicated to the quest for a perfect filet, that ideal bottle of wine, and the hugest baked potatoes ever pulled from Idaho's soil. This first-rate beef heaven ages each of its cuts 21 days before serving, and the results are nothing short of magnificent. It's a fine place, even if it's located inside one of Vegas's zooiest casino hotels, and no one blinks if you show up in casual clothes. True to its name, **El Gaucho** (in the Tropicana) fixes meats with either the traditional grill treatment or with an Argentinean blend of marinades and herbs. If you'd rather go somewhere close to the Strip but not inside a casino hotel, try **Morton's of Chicago**, a branch of the national steak-house chain, at Fashion Square Mall. The serious atmosphere at this overpriced and pseudo-clubby spot may make you temporarily forget about Vegas's penchant for frivolity. The always busy **Golden Steer** has been in business since Nixon was in the White House (and in this town, that's a stand-up testimonial to a place's quality and service). Being only a block from the convention center, it regularly fills up with conventioneers, but otherwise it's a local business hangout. If you like lobster fra diavolo, a standard dish on Vegas seafood/steak-house menus, order it here: The Golden Steer's is second to none. Another very worthwhile steak-house choice is **The Palm** (inside the Fashion Court at Caesars), a Vegas outpost of what many consider to be the nation's most consistent and successful chain of high-end steak houses. The Palm's one of those spots that takes itself way, way too seriously, with its walls filled with celebrity photos, autographed murals, and the like. But then again, it delivers consistently luscious meat and perfectly done side dishes. Off the Strip, there's **Yolie's Brazilian Steakhouse**, an unusual place that roasts its meats "rodizio style" inside a glass rotisserie, marinating and herbing them to heavenly perfection, and serving everything alongside feijoada (black bean and beef stew). If you really want a whale of a good time, eat here during Mardi Gras, that season when Brazilians all over the world do their wildest living. **Billy Bob's Steakhouse** at Sam's Town is the place to go not only for decent, inexpensive steaks, but also for Rocky Mountain oysters: deep-fried bull testicles dipped in shrimp-cocktail sauce. For the uninitiated, Rocky Mountain oysters manage to be greasy and crunchy at the same time, sort of like bad fried chicken. Sounds awful, tastes great.

Romance... If wining, dining, and shining is at the top of your priorities list, head over to **Mortoni's**, the northern Italian restaurant tucked in the back reaches of the Hard Rock Hotel. Built to satisfy the dining needs of Peter Morton, the Hard Rock's hard-driving owner, Mortoni's is a very sophisticated restaurant decked out with a sleek, urbane look. Its view of the Hard Rock's pool area is great, as is the restaurant's liberal use of blond woods and hand-sculpted sconces. Oh, and the food's great, in large part because Mr. Morton makes sure it stays affordable and unpretentious. Come here for pasta dishes laced with fragrant spices of the Southwest (the chef cut her culinary teeth at Santa Fe's Coyote Cafe), as well as Mama Morton's Chicago-style lasagne and Pete's favorite antipasto. **Andiamo**, inside the Las Vegas Hilton, is a first-rate northern Italian restaurant with an uneven staff—they have a tendency to ignore the fine points of service. But it's still a great setting for a romantic evening, mainly because the food is so delicious—*rigatoni con melanzane* (tube pasta with eggplant), *lasagne de polenta con salsiccia* (lasagne with polenta and sausage), as well as a dozen or so different veal and lamb specialties, and a dessert called *sogno di Venizia*, a chocolate gondola filled with white espresso gelato. The huge wine list is heavily slanted toward Italian varietals. **Rosewood Grille** has all the right decor touches for romance—dark wood paneling, red carpets, white table linens—and upscale menu selections like a perfect six-ounce filet mignon or a delicate grilled fillet of Pacific tuna. Rosewood even jets 10-pound lobsters straight from Maine's coastal fisheries into Vegas; it's one of the few places on earth where you can drop $150 on a seafood dinner—and in this town, that's half a ticket to Maui! The Mirage's **Moongate** does a fantastic job of capturing the spirit of an evening in Beijing; from the moat surrounding its entrance to the Forbidden City decor, once you're inside Moongate you may as well be eight time zones away from the Strip. And in true imperial fashion, the menu is priced too high for the masses.

Mucho gusto... Though it may not occur to you at first, Las Vegas *is* part of the Southwest, and Mexican immigration has brought large numbers of hard-working, Spanish-speaking people across the border to work in behind-the-scenes jobs (construction, hotel housekeeping, restaurant cooking) to make your Vegas experience possible. And, like all the Southwest, Las Vegas is blessed with many wonderful Mexican restaurants, either owned by Mexican immigrants or patronized primarily by Mexican and Chicano locals. The most authentic Mexican dining experience in Vegas is at **Lindo Michoacan**, a neighborhood bar and restaurant serving stiff margaritas, a homemade salsa with lots of ground red chile, and a muy bueno *menudo* (a traditional soup made from tripe, chiles, and hominy) on weekends. At the Fiesta casino hotel is **Garduno's Cantina**, a branch of the famous Albuquerque restaurant; here you can sink your teeth into first-rate enchiladas, fajitas, and tamales, though they do tone down the chile pepper quotient for Vegas visitors' wimpier palates. Another great neighborhood place is **Doña María's**, a downtown spot known for its homemade tamales and great happy hours with freebie Mexican finger foods. In the casino hotels on the Strip, check out the Stardust's **Tres Lobos**, which has a long-standing reputation as the best Mexican restaurant on the Strip. Its hacienda-like decor is a suitable setting for traditional dishes like chimichangas and rolled enchiladas; its selection of a dozen or so Mexican beers encourages you to branch out beyond Dos Equis. Bally's **Las Olas** has the Strip's most elegant decor for a Mexican restaurant, but it's got more of a Tex-Mex menu, serving huge platters of tacos, burritos, and tostadas, layered with mounds of refried beans and smothered in grated cheddar cheese. Just off the Strip is **Margaritagrille** at the Las Vegas Hilton, where the Santa Fe–style decor has gone far over the top. The kitchen's creative urges seem to have run wild in ways that are very un-Mexicano, but they do add a lighter touch, incorporating items like crab enchiladas, ceviche, shrimp fajitas, and low-cal flans, which are all highly recommended. The city's best fajita restaurant, the **Guadalajara Grille** at Palace Station casino hotel, has a very authentic take on Mexican street fare. With perfect tableside service, the staff will grind guacamole as you watch; the kitchen also dishes up a wickedly hot *pico de gallo* (a jalapeño-loaded salsa) and makes tortillas right on the premises.

Cosi fan tutti... Italian restaurants are far and away Vegas's most popular type of dining spot—you'll be hard pressed to drive more than a few blocks without running across at least a few pizza, pasta, and veal joints. Off the Strip, the city's standard for Italian restaurants was set decades ago by the **Venetian Ristorante**, a place that's almost as funky on its muraled inside as it is on its muraled outside. The Venetian will warm the soul of any paisano longing for home, with its old-style menu, gray-haired waitresses, and unusual dishes like marinated pork neck bones with pepperoncini (ask for extra bread to sop up the rich sauce). A more contemporary interpretation of Italian cuisine is the attraction at the nearby **North Beach Cafe**, a fantastic and innovative pasta temple with reasonable prices. Lawyers and businesspeople have made the Vegas outpost of **Romano's Macaroni Grill**, a chain based in San Antonio, a big success. They no doubt appreciate the quick-as-lightning service here, but the food is also dependably authentic, if safely middle-of-the-road, and the crusty Italian bread served with all the meals is nothing short of fantastic. **Strings Italian Cafe**, on the east side of town, is a pleasant, neighborhood type of place with a menu that sticks to standards—eggplant parmagiana, veggie lasagne, and spinach linguine with red clam sauce. If you're down by the Strip, stop in at **Battista's Pizza Rio**, a quiet, wood-paneled hangout for casino execs snatching an hour of relief from the clang-clang of slots and poker machines. The very reasonably priced menu includes standards like sausage-and-pepper wedges, baked ziti, and minestrone soup, all prepared from scratch. On the Strip, one of my favorite spaghetti-and-a-glass-of-Chianti places is the Riviera's **Ristorante Italiano**, which is simple, unpretentious, and cheap, if not exactly the best Italian food you'll find in town. Mirage's **Ristorante Riva** is another good bet, though its northern Italian menu is, like the rest of the Mirage, on the pricy side. But Caesars Palace's **Primavera** is probably the best of the Strip's more straightforward attempts at Italian dining: This poolside trattoria is best known for its pasta dishes, though the menu covers the full range of Italian foods. If any restaurant in town has a better setting than **Bertolini's**, right at the edge of the Fountain of the Gods inside the Forum Shops, I've yet to see it; the people-watching here is simply the best in town. The fairly standard pastas, pizzas, and desserts served at too-high prices won't draw much more than tourists to Bertolini's, but there's nothing wrong with coming here just for the chance to see who struts what in and out of the Forum Shops' expensive boutiques. For a real change of pace try the romantic setting at **Pampios Italian Kitchen** at Sam's Town, a fairly standard though cozy cafe where your table is set outside in an air-conditioned, tree-shaded park filled with waterfalls and birds—a welcome relief from the Vegas desert environment. The menu at Pampios sticks to standards like linguine Alfredo, veal marsala, and tiramisu; the main attraction here is the ersatz-forest setting. And if you couldn't make it to the Liberace Museum (which closes daily at 5pm), here's the next best thing: **Carluccio's Tivoli Gardens**. Located in the same shopping plaza as the museum, this restaurant was started by Liberace himself (it was originally called Liberace's Tivoli Gardens) in tribute to his adored Italian mother. The kitchen does a good enough job with standards from the basic Italian cookbook (lobster fra diavolo, cannoli, osso bucco, etc.), but what really makes it memorable are the glittering Liberace decor, piano, and attitudes.

Taking care of business... If you're here for a convention and need someplace to put the Strip behind you for a few hours, try **Cafe Michelle West**, a favorite of the city's business set. Cafe Michelle's screened patios are filled with power-lunchers from April through October; the rest of the year, these same folks just head inside to the cafe's rustic dining room for their see-and-be-seen scene. The very popular **Fog City Diner** on the east side of the Strip is another place that will impress your guests, primarily because it successfully combines the light approach of Californian food interpretations with more down-to-earth standards such as mashed potatoes, grilled seasonal veggies, and innovative desserts. Locals have always favored **The Tillerman**'s spacious, multiroom interior for business lunches; its handy location right off the Strip's east side (close to the convention center) is a major reason to seal that big deal here. Downtown, the top choice is **André's**, a quiet and very Continental sort of place that's made its reputation as a hangout for discreet movers and shakers; its interior is filled with just the sort of nooks and crannies that are perfect for confidential conversations. If you can't get away from the Strip, try the Las Vegas Hilton's **Bistro Le Montrachet**, which is within walking distance of the convention center. The subdued Parisian-bistro atmosphere and discreet staff help business conversations stay on track, while the classic French cuisine adds a note of sophistication. Of course, if your expense account can handle it, there are always those $200 bottles of Chateau Lafitte on the wine list.

LATE NIGHT DINING ⟨ THE LOWDOWN

The Index

$$$$	$40 and over
$$$	$20–$40
$$	$10–$20
$	under $10

Prices reflect the cost of dinner per person, not including drinks, tax, or tip. All restaurants are open daily unless otherwise noted.

Andiamo. Wonderful northern Italian food, decent enough ambience, but indifferent service.... *Tel 702/732–5111. 3000 Paradise Rd. Open until 11pm. $$$*

André's. Downtown's standard for elegance in Continental dining, André's has the city's best wine list, most powerful old-money crowd, and prices to match.... *Tel 702/385–5016. 401 S. 6th St. Open until 11pm. $$$$*

Bacchanal. Legendary dining experience within the Caesars complex, Bacchanal is an expensive, fixed-price restaurant where diners are served by centurions and goddesses.... *Tel 702/731–7731. Caesars Palace, 3570 Las Vegas Blvd. S. Open until midnight; last seating at 9:30pm. $$$$*

Battista's Pizza Rio. Family-operated Italian restaurant offers first-rate pizza in a friendly setting. It also has pizza to go.... *Tel 702/733–3950. 4041 Audrie St. Open until 11pm, Sun until 8pm. $*

Beach Cafe. Trying hard to grab the lion's share of Vegas's all-night breakfast crowd, the Beach Cafe's claim to fame is a T-bone steak dinner for just $2.99 (served 11pm to 7am), as well as several other terrific breakfast specials under $4.... *Tel 702/252–7777. Rio Suites, 3700 W. Flamingo Rd. Open 24 hours. $*

Benihana. Tried-and-true outpost of teppan-style Japanese tableside cooking. Benihana's Vegas location is as fresh as they come.... *Tel 702/732–5111. Las Vegas Hilton, 3000 Paradise Rd. Open until 11pm. $$$*

Bertolini's. Passable Italian fare, served in front of the faux Trevi Fountain inside the Forum Shops.... *Tel 702/735–4663. Caesars Palace, 3500 Las Vegas Blvd. S. Open until 11pm. $$*

Billy Bob's Steakhouse. Like everything else at Sam's Town, good quality at fantastic prices.... *Tel 702/456–7777. Sam's Town, 5111 Boulder Hwy. Open until 11pm. $$*

Binion's Horseshoe. To glimpse what this town was like before the corporate-owned casinos moved in, sidle over to this very friendly, never pretentious downtown casino hotel. Buffet, sandwich bar, and steak deals all served in the same cafe.... *Tel 702/382–1600. Binion's Horseshoe, 128 E. Fremont St. Open until 10:30pm. $*

Bistro Le Montrachet. With its sophisticated French setting, this is a good place to ink that huge deal you negotiated at the convention.... *Tel 702/732–5111. Las Vegas Hilton, 3000 Paradise Rd. Open until 10:30pm. $$$$*

Cafe Nicolle. Favorite place for the city's movers and shakers. The piano bar is filled with Armani suits every evening at 5pm for a yuppie happy hour, and its shaded patio, cooled off with artificial mist, does an amazing lunch business.... *Tel 702/870–7675. 4760 W. Sahara Ave. Open until 11pm. $$$*

Cafe Michelle West. Vegas's hottest place for cutting a business deal, Cafe Michelle offers live entertainment on weekends, a piano bar on weeknights, and a power-brokers' lunch atmosphere on its huge patios.... *Tel 702/873–5400. 2800 W. Sahara Ave. Open until 11pm. $$$*

Camelot. Quiet, wood-paneled elegance and reasonable prices make Camelot one of the Strip's best gourmet-room bargains.... *Tel 702/597–7449. Excalibur, 3850 Las Vegas Blvd. S. Open until 11pm. $$*

Carluccio's Tivoli Gardens. Originally founded by Liberace, this is a magnet for Liberace lovers and pasta nibblers. Guess whose music plays in the background?.... *Tel 702/*

795–3236. 1775 E. Tropicana Ave. Open Tue–Sun until 10pm. Closed Mon. $$

Carnival World Buffet. Hands down, the best buffet in Vegas—count on insanely long lines no matter what time of day or night.... Tel 702/252–7777. Rio Suites, 3700 W. Flamingo Rd. Open until 11pm. $

Circus Circus Buffet. The name says it all: Kids and families are more than welcome, they're catered to at this aging but highly profitable casino hotel. The buffet line is always crowded with large families, large people, and large groups searching for unlimited food at a bargain price.... Tel 702/734–0410. Circus Circus, 2880 Las Vegas Blvd. S. Open until 11pm. $

Country Star. Rub shoulders with photos of country music's high and mighty, buy some stuff, say "Howdy!" to the waitpersons.... Tel 702/740–8400. 3770 Las Vegas Blvd. S. Open until midnight. $$

Coyote Cafe. Southwestern elegance at its best, in Santa Fe star chef Mark Miller's very popular restaurant.... Tel 702/ 891–7349. MGM Grand, 3799 Las Vegas Blvd. S. Open until 11pm. $$$

Dive. Bring your kids here for a glimpse of what Spielberg's mind can do with a few million extra bucks and some cooks who know how to do burgers.... Tel 702/369–3483. 3200 Las Vegas Blvd. S. Open until midnight, weekends until 1am. $

Doña Maria's. Famous for its homemade tamales, this downtown Mexican restaurant hosts a super-crowded happy hour, when pitchers of margaritas flow and the mariachis play.... Tel 702/ 382–6538. 910 Las Vegas Blvd. S. Open until 10pm. $$

Dragon Noodle Company. Fresh and inexpensive alternative to the Strip's Asian restaurants.... Tel 702/891–7331. Monte Carlo, 3770 Las Vegas Blvd. S. Open Mon–Thur until 10pm, Fri–Sat until midnight. $$

El Gaucho. Steak house with a Latin flair.... Tel 702/739–2222. Tropicana, 3801 Las Vegas Blvd. S. Open until 11pm. $$

Emeril's. The latest entrant in this city's battle of celebrity chefs, Emeril's serves up fantastic service, great seafood, and non-stop innovations, New Orleans–style.... *Tel 702/891–7374. MGM Grand, 3799 Las Vegas Blvd. S. Open until 11pm. $$$*

Emperor's Room. This downtown casino hotel's Chinese restaurant is a throwback to the days before Szechuan food made a dent on America's culinary psyche.... *Tel 702/477–3000. Lady Luck, 206 N. 3rd St. Open until 11pm. $*

Festival Buffet. This North Las Vegas casino hotel keeps things on a small scale—a perfect reason to flee from the Strip. Great desserts, a gourmet coffee bar, pleasant setting, and decent prices (but not the cheapest).... *Tel 702/631–7000. Fiesta, 2400 N. Rancho Dr. Open until 10pm. $*

Fiore. Classy European-style gourmet room with wood-fired ovens and French chefs.... *Tel 702/252–7702. Rio Suites, 3700 W. Flamingo Rd. Open until midnight. $$$$*

Fog City Diner. Fantastic quality, innovative menu, cool decor, and great waitstaff.... *Tel 702/737–0200. 325 Hughes Center Dr. Open until 11pm. $$$*

Garduno's Cantina. Vegas outpost of one of New Mexico's most popular family dining spots, Garduno's is known for its great fajitas, killer margaritas, and low prices.... *Tel 702/631–7000. Fiesta, 2400 N. Rancho Dr. Open until 11pm. $$*

Gatsby's. One of the Strip's best gourmet rooms, known for great wines, high prices, and Rockefeller-meets-Hollywood decor.... *Tel 702/891–7777. MGM Grand, 3799 Las Vegas Blvd. S. Open until midnight (last seating 9:30pm). $$$$*

Gold Coast. Off the Strip, this friendly casino hotel has a great buffet (snag that free drink) and other incredible meal deals.... *Tel 702/367–7111. Gold Coast, 4000 W. Flamingo Rd. Open until 10pm. $*

Golden Nugget. Where to find 99-cent shrimp cocktails in a civilized setting. Be sure to check out the international beer bar as you walk through the casino's doors.... *Tel 702/385–7111. Golden Nugget, 129 E. Fremont St. Open until 10pm. $*

Golden Steer. Dating from the 1960s (that's ancient for Vegas), it's still a favorite with locals for its prime ribs, Iowa beef steaks, and down-home friendliness. Regularly fills up with conventioneers; otherwise, it's a local business hangout.... *Tel 702/384–4470. 308 W. Sahara Ave. Open until 11:30pm. $$*

Guadalajara Grille. Very authentic and popular Mexican restaurant serving Vegas's best fajitas and hottest salsas.... *Tel 702/367–2411. Palace Station, 2411 W. Sahara Ave. Open until 11pm. $$*

Hamada of Japan. Favored late-night hangout for showgirls and dancers working production shows on the nearby Strip, Hamada has one of the cleanest and friendliest sushi bars anywhere.... *Tel 702/733–3005. 598 E. Flamingo Rd. Open until 2am. $$$*

Hard Rock Cafe. Buy a T-shirt, act too cool, and join the hordes at the Hard Rock.... *Tel 702/733–8400. 4475 Paradise Rd. Open until midnight. $$*

Iron Horse Cafe. Locals like the off-Strip location of these two casino hotel cafes, which makes parking easier and the atmosphere much friendlier. Solid reputation for good food at affordable prices, but not much on ambience.... *Tel 702/432–7777, Boulder Station, 4111 Boulder Hwy; tel 702/367–2411, Palace Station, 2411 W. Sahara Ave. Open 24 hours. $*

Isis. This gourmet room is decorated to look like King Tut's tomb (or maybe just his rec room). Feast like a pharaoh for a king's ransom.... *Tel 702/262–4000. Luxor, 3900 Las Vegas Blvd S. Open until 11pm. $$$$*

Kabuki Japanese Restaurant. Low-priced sushi in a slightly tacky atmosphere. Unfriendly staff and inattention to detail make this a poor choice for anyone wanting uncooked fish.... *Tel 702/733–0066. 1150 E. Twain Ave. Open until 11pm. $$*

Kady's. An all-night coffee shop serving inexpensive specials after 11pm. Nothing going for it in the way of decor.... *Tel 702/734–5110. Riviera, 2901 Las Vegas Blvd. S. Open 24 hours. $*

Komol Thai. The city's best spot for pad Thai, this favorite of Las Vegas's growing Asian community is also an offbeat weekend choice for live entertainment.... *Tel 702/731–6542. 453 E. Sahara Ave. Open until 11pm. $$*

Las Olas. Nicely decorated hotel joint, always good for a fix of cheesy Tex-Mex food.... *Tel 702/739–4111. Bally's 3645 Las Vegas Blvd. S. Open until 11pm. $$*

Lilly Langtry's. Has been and continues to reign as downtown's most elegant Asian restaurant.... *Tel 702/386–8131. Golden Nugget, 129 E. Fremont St. Open until 11pm. $$$*

Lindo Michoacan. The most authentic Mexican food in town is served at this family-run operation a few miles east of the Strip. Margaritas are first rate, as are the huevos rancheros.... *Tel 702/735–6828. 2655 E. Desert Inn Rd. Open until 10pm, Fri–Sat until 11pm. $$*

Lookout Cafe. Greatest place in Vegas to catch the frigate battle taking place nightly in Treasure Island's lagoon.... *Tel 702/894–7111. Treasure Island, 3300 Las Vegas Blvd. S. Open 24 hours. $*

Magical Empire. Another of Caesars's dining adventures, this one transports you into the casino's underworld for a dinner and magic show featuring several illusionists and a fantastic stage set.... *Tel 702/731–7324. Caesars Palace, 3570 Las Vegas Blvd S. Open until 11:30pm. $$$$*

Magnolia's Verandah Cafe. The cafe at Four Queens turns into Vegas's best jazz club during its Monday night jam sessions, when you can hang around this classic downtown joint soakin' up the jazzmen's vibes.... *Tel 702/385–4011. Four Queens, 202 E. Fremont St. Open 24 hours. $*

Margaritagrille. Interesting and innovative interpretations of traditional Mexican dishes; overdone Santa Fe–style decor.... *Tel 702/732–5111. Las Vegas Hilton, 3000 Paradise Rd. Open until 11pm. $$*

Market Place Buffet. One of the Strip's best bargains, the Aladdin's buffet is priced just a few bucks higher than Circus Circus's, providing a margin of insurance from the buffet locusts.... *Tel 702/736–0111. Aladdin, 3667 Las Vegas Blvd. S. Open until 10pm. $*

Market Street Buffet. One big reason Vegas locals like the buffet here is its emphasis on grilled and barbecued meats;

LATE NIGHT DINING ✐ *THE INDEX*

its fajita stand and Chinese noodle shop are popular, too.... *Tel 702/631–1000. Texas Station, 2101 Texas Star Lane. Open until 10pm. $*

Mikado. Japanese fine dining, to complement the Chinese cuisine offered at its sister restaurant, the Moongate.... *Tel 702/791–7111. Mirage, 3400 Las Vegas Blvd. S. Open until 11pm. $$$*

Ming Terrace. Trying to look authentic, this Asian-esque restaurant goes way over the top in its decor, but the meal makes it worth it—great quality, wide range of selections, and friendly service.... *Tel 702/794–3261. Imperial Palace, 3535 Las Vegas Blvd. S. Open until midnight, Fri–Sat until 1am. $$*

Mizuno's Teppan Dining. Great chefs cooking tableside with lotsa flair and a few Vegas-style jokes. Grab a sake and join the fun.... *Tel 702/739–2713. Tropicana, 3801 Las Vegas Blvd. S. Open until 10:45pm. $$*

Moongate. This enchanting journey into Asian dining keeps pace with the Mirage's steady stream of Asian high rollers.... *Tel 702/791–7111. Mirage, 3400 Las Vegas Blvd. S. Open until 11pm. $$$*

Morton's of Chicago. Vegas outpost of the Chicago-based steak-house chain.... *Tel 702/893–0703. Fashion Square Mall, 3200 Las Vegas Blvd. S. Open until 11pm. $$$*

Mortoni's. Affordable and ultra-cool Italian restaurant facing onto the Hard Rock's pool, one of Vegas's most dependably beautiful sights.... *Tel 702/693–5000. Hard Rock Hotel, 4455 Paradise Rd. Open until 11pm. $$*

Mr. Lucky's 24/7. The coolest place in Vegas for all-night hanging out, loaded with celebs, models, musicians, and a young, monied breed of tourist. The food is as hip as the atmosphere, too.... *Tel 702/ 693–5000. Hard Rock Hotel, 4455 Paradise Rd. Open 24 hours. $$*

North Beach Cafe. Hung with local art, this popular pasta spot makes waves in the city's business world.... *Tel 702/247–9530. 2605 S. Decatur Blvd. Open until 10pm. $$$*

Oz Buffet. One of the Strip's best buffet bargains, the Oz Buffet does things in a typically overscale style, yet doesn't lose sight of quality.... *Tel 702/891–1111. MGM Grand, 3799 Las Vegas Blvd. S. Open until 10pm. $*

Palace Court. Pricey Continental and American standards, executed to perfection.... *Tel 702/731–7110. Caesars Palace, 3570 Las Vegas Blvd. S. Open until 11pm. $$$$*

Palatium Buffet. Highest buffet prices on the Strip, and probably one of the top buffets, too.... *Tel 702/731–7110. Caesars Palace, 3570 Las Vegas Blvd. S. Open until 10pm. $$*

The Palm. The nation's best steak-house chain has its Vegas branch inside the Forum Shops.... *Tel 702/732–7254. Caesars Palace, 3570 Las Vegas Blvd. S. Open until 11pm. $$$*

Pamplos Italian Kitchen. Reliable, if not especially inspired, northern Italian cuisine served in an enclosed outdoor theme park at Sam's Town.... *Tel 702/456–7777. 5111 Boulder Hwy. Open until 11pm. $$*

Papyrus. Elegant take on Polynesian dining in a quiet corner of the Luxor's mezzanine.... *Tel 702/262–4000. Luxor, 3900 Las Vegas Blvd. S. Open until 11pm. $$$*

Paradise Buffet. The Fremont's buffet has good quality, low prices, and a Friday seafood feast that's worth driving across town for.... *Tel 702/385–3232. Fremont, 200 E. Fremont St. Open until 10pm, Fri until 11pm. $*

Planet Hollywood. Movie-themed paraphernalia boutique with California casual food on the side. Stand in line.... *Tel 702/ 791–7827. 3500 Las Vegas Blvd. S. Open until 2am. $$*

Primavera. This northern Italian restaurant can seat you facing the pool, which is usually loaded with gods and goddesses.... *Tel 702/731–7731. Caesars Palace, 3570 Las Vegas Blvd. S. Open until 11pm. $$*

Ristorante Italiano. Simple and straightforward Italian spaghetti house inside the Riviera.... *Tel 702/734–5110. Riviera, 2901 Las Vegas Blvd. S. Open until 11pm. $$*

Ristorante Riva. Catering to an international high-roller set, this pasta house charges high prices for not-so-special dishes.... *Tel 702/791–7111. Mirage, 3400 Las Vegas Blvd. S. Open until 11pm. $$$*

Romano's Macaroni Grill. Off the Strip, get an inexpensive Italian meal at this Vegas outpost of a fast-growing national chain. High quality, fun atmosphere, and very family friendly.... *Tel 702/248–9500. 2400 W. Sahara Ave. Open until 11pm. $$*

Rosewood Grille. This elegant Strip restaurant serves fantastic steaks, scampi, lobster, etc.... *Tel 702/792–9099. 3339 Las Vegas Blvd. S. Open until 11:30pm. $$$$*

Seasons. One of the Strip's best gourmet rooms, with all the important details: elegant silverware, linen tablecloths, friendly waiters, and a superb wine list. The menu emphasizes whatever's fresh that day from vendors around the world.... *Tel 702/739–4651. Bally's, 3645 Las Vegas Blvd. S. Open until 11pm. $$$$*

Sir Galahad's. Lotsa beef, low prices, and waitpersons dressed like extras in *Braveheart* (not the ones fighting on Mel Gibson's side) have made Sir Galahad's one of the Strip's busiest prime-rib houses.... *Tel 702/597–7777. Excalibur, 3850 Las Vegas Blvd. S. Open until 11pm. $$*

Sisters Cafe & Grille. A good place to grab a meal in the middle of the night, with live music until the wee hours.... *Tel 702/380–7777. Stratosphere, 2000 Las Vegas Blvd. S. Open 24 hours. $*

Smokey Joe's Cafe. Country-market atmosphere and outstanding specials keep locals coming back to this Boulder Strip cafe.... *Tel 702/456-7777. Sam's Town, 5111 Boulder Hwy. Open 24 hours. $*

Spago. Celeb-chef Wolfgang Puck's entry into Vegas's high-end restaurant sweepstakes. Great pizzas, people-watching, and star-gazing in the Forum Shops.... *Tel 702/369–6300. Caesars Palace, 3570 Las Vegas Blvd. S. Open until 10pm, weekends until 10:30. $$$*

The Steak House. An old-money setting just inside a pair of walnut doors that separate The Steak House from this casino hotel's usual madness.... *Tel 702/794–3767. Circus Circus, 2880 Las Vegas Blvd. S. Open until midnight. $$$*

Strings Italian Cafe. Simple, neighborhood-type Italian restaurant with lasagne, pasta, some chicken dishes, and lotsa families.... *Tel 702/739–6400. 2222 E. Tropicana Blvd. Open until 10pm, Fri–Sat until 11pm. $$*

The Tillerman. For years, the city's most popular upscale seafood restaurant. A great place for business lunches, romantic dinners, and dressing up to see and be seen.... *Tel 702/731–4036. 2245 E. Flamingo Rd. Open until 11pm. $$$*

Togoshi Ramen. First-rate Japanese noodle house with amazingly low prices and astoundingly banal decor.... *Tel 702/737–7003. 855 E. Twain Ave. Open until 11pm. $*

Top of the World. This gourmet room has one thing going for it nobody can match: a 360-degree, rotating view from 1,000 feet above the Strip.... *Tel 702/380–7777. Statosphere, 2000 Las Vegas Blvd. S. Open until 11pm, weekends until midnight. $$$*

Treasure Island Buffet. Family-oriented buffet with a boffo view of Treasure Island's pirate-battle show.... *Tel 702/894–7111. Treasure Island, 3300 Las Vegas Blvd. S. Open until 11pm. $*

Tres Lobos. Mexican restaurant set in hacienda-like decor, known for low prices, huge portions, and big eaters.... *Tel 702/732–6111. Stardust, 3000 Las Vegas Blvd. S. Open until 11pm. $*

Venetian Ristorante. The most authentic neighborhood-style Italian restaurant in Vegas. Dress up nice, but don't put on airs.... *Tel 702/876–4190. 3713 W. Sahara Ave. Open until 11pm, Fri–Sat until midnight. $$$*

Yolie's Brazilian Steakhouse. Famous for rotisserie-grilled meats.... *Tel 702/794–0700. 3900 Paradise Rd. Open until 11pm. $$$*

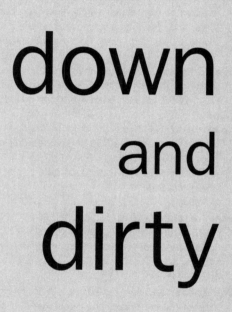

down
and
dirty

All-night pharmacies... For 24-hour pharmaceutical necessities, try **White Cross Drugs** (tel 702/382–1733; 1700 Las Vegas Blvd. S.) or **Sav-on Drugs** (tel 702/731–5373, 800/627–2866; 1360 E. Flamingo Rd.; other locations around town).

Babysitters... Concierges at the larger hotels can recommend experienced, reliable babysitting services or child-care nurseries. Some babysitting services have facilities located close to the Strip, where kids can be dropped off and picked up at any hour. One of the most reliable is **Around the Clock Child Care** (tel 702/365–1040, 800/798–6768), which lives up to its name and never seems fazed by any request from a high roller with a stroller. If your hotel doesn't offer concierge service, and the front desk staff is unable to make a recommendation, just call one of the larger casino hotels and ask for the concierge desk: these people are so darn friendly and helpful, they'll give you the info you need even if you're not staying there.

Car rentals... All major car rental agencies have airport locations. Agencies in town include **Advantage** (tel 702/386–5775); **Agency** (tel 702/871–8508, 800/321–1972); **Alamo** (tel 702/263–3030, 800/327–9633); **Allstate** (tel 702/736–6147); **Avis** (tel 702/261–5595, 800/331–1212); **Budget** (tel 702/736–1212, 800/527–0700); **Dollar** (tel 702/739–8408, 800/800–4000); **Enterprise** (tel 702/795–8842); **Hertz** (tel 702/735–4900, 800/654–3131); **National** (tel 702/261–5391, 800/227–7368); **Rent-a-Vette** (tel 702/736–2592); **Snappy** (tel 702/739–0200); **Thrifty** (tel 702/896–7600, 800/367–2277); and **Value** (tel 702/733–8886).

Driving around... The city is laid out in a simple grid pattern with a few one-way streets and lots of turn lanes on both the right- and left-hand sides of major roads. Your car rental agency will provide you with a simple map of the city's streets, but if you want a map with more detail, your best bet is to buy one at one of the hundreds of gas station–minimart operations lining Vegas's streets. Gas is relatively cheap—unless you take advantage (or are taken advantage of by) the video-poker and slot machines at every filling station. Vegas has the usual rush hours early in the morning and late in the afternoon, but the Strip's worst traffic occurs on weekend nights, when tens of thousands of tourists and high-school kids insist on cruising from the Stratosphere to the Luxor causing bumper-to-bumper crawls. The best way to negotiate Strip gridlock is to do as locals do and limit your driving to the north-south streets running parallel to the Strip. On the east side of the Strip, try Paradise Road and Koval Lane; on the west side, take Industrial Road. Every casino hotel has an access point on the side road closest to its rear entrance.

Emergencies... To reach local **ambulances**, the **fire department**, or the **police**, dial 911. Hospitals include **Desert Springs Hospital** (tel 702/733–8800; 2075 E. Flamingo Rd.); **Columbia Sunrise Hospital** (tel 702/ 255–5000; 3100 N. Tenaya Way); and the **University Medical Center** (tel 702/383–2000; 1800 W. Charleston Blvd.). All of these have emergency rooms.

Festivals and special events... Las Vegas doesn't lay on special events like other cities do—why cook up literary festivals, holiday parades, or ethnic celebrations when the town is already a non-stop party? But there is one thing you'll need to contend with when scheduling a trip to Las Vegas: conventions. Over the last decade, the Las Vegas Convention and Visitors Authority has been extraordinarily successful in booking up the 1.6-million-square-foot Las Vegas Convention Center on Paradise Road; each year, more than 3,000,000 conventioneers are whisked in and out of Las Vegas. For the convention planner, Vegas's advantages are obvious: cheap room rates, cheap food, warm weather, and, of course, the all-night action. And with nearly 100,000 hotel rooms, Las Vegas has the capacity to absorb swarms of conventioneers. Many of these groups only tie up a few hundred rooms at a time, but there are some truly humongous gatherings you should try to schedule your trip around. Among these are January's Consumer Electronics Show, April's convocation of the National Association of Broadcasters, and COMDEX, a gargantuan computer show, in Novermber. If you're a rodeo fan, come to town in December, when 10,000 cowpokes and hordes more of their fans crowd into town for the National Rodeo Finals—expect the Strip to be clogged with 2-ton pick-ups hauling horse trailers.

Besides conventions, a few other mega-events tend to clog things up—world championship prizefights, major rodeos, and concerts by big-name groups like the Stones or Pearl Jam. As for the Super Bowl, it may well be the biggest unofficial convention of all, as a backslapping rabble of bookies and tip-sheet operators converge here for football action. If you're having some trouble making hotel reservations for the days you want to visit Vegas, ask the reservation clerk if there's a conflict with a large event or convention in town. If that's the case, being a little creative with your dates could open things up for you.

Limousines... The casino hotels won't send their limos to pick you up unless you're a known high roller, but **Bell Trans** (tel 702/739–7990) shared-ride limos can drive you in and out of McCarran at any hour of the day or night, allowing you to arrive at the hotel's entrance in high-roller style. Call a day or so ahead to reserve your limo; it'll cost you $3.50 to the Strip, $4.75 to downtown.

Magazines... The city's two best freebie publications (a k a "alternative rags") are the weekly *New Times* and the monthly *Scope* (see "Sources," in The Arts). One of the wackier freebie weekly publications is *L.V.M.S.* (*Las Vegas Music Scene*), which covers the city's blues, heavy metal, and rock bands. With its slapped-together appearance, *L.V.M.S.* looks like the kind of publication only a follower of the local music scene would read, but it's actually the city's best source for information about up-and-coming acts playing neighborhood bars, as well as the older mojo men working the city's smallish blues scene. Three slickly produced freebie magazines are distributed throughout hotel rooms, coffee bars, and record stores. *Showbiz Weekly* and *What's On in Las Vegas* both offer tips and general info for everyone from hicks to sharpies. *What's On* is independently owned, while *Showbiz* is cranked out by the *Las Vegas Sun*, the afternoon newspaper. Crammed with ads from casinos, tour companies, retailers, and restaurants, *Showbiz* primarily features uncritical previews of upcoming acts (there's also a horoscope section that predicts your gambling luck). Stressing calendar listings above editorial content, *What's On* has practically the same target audience as *Showbiz*, but devotes more coverage to the Strip's live-music scene, and adds insider tips for the gambling tables. Though it isn't distributed as widely as *What's On* or *Showbiz*, the surprisingly useful *Today in Las Vegas* is a weekly, pamphlet-sized glossy with a more independent, objective voice on matters such as restaurants, production shows, concerts, and lounge acts. *Today* is strongest on useful tourist tips: tennis courts, golf courses, places of worship, wedding chapels, and family attractions are all duly covered, making this an indispensable information source for the visitor who wants to go beyond the Strip. The quarterly **Las Vegas Magazine** and the monthly **Las Vegas Style Magazine** are two glossies that cover the city's entertainment scene; *Las Vegas Style* plays up (and panders to) Las Vegas's glitzy side, while *Las Vegas Magazine* adopts a more serious approach to the city's arts, restaurant, and society scenes. The city's gaming industry has its own publications (in addition to the news coverage it receives in the *Review-Journal*'s business pages). **Casino Journal** is a slick, large-format monthly that provides an overview of the entire gaming industry, from Native American casinos in the Northeast to the latest plans for expanding casino hotels on the Strip. Weekly **Gaming Today** serves as something of a mouthpiece for corporate pronouncements from the casino hotel industry, but it also contains loads of advice on how to maximize your chances of winning in certain gaming situations, as well as information on sports betting, local restaurants, and Las Vegas entertainment. You can also find some minimal assistance on gambling techniques in the monthly **Casino Player**, as well as in the quarterly **Casino Games**, which is more oriented toward the beginning gambler. *Casino Games* also offers entertainment listings, but there's more feature coverage of the city's nightlife and dining scenes in *Casino Player*. Disregard the prices printed on their covers: Both are distributed free in hotels, gift shops, bookstores, and visitor centers.

Parking... You have two options when parking your car at most casino hotels, both of them free. Valet parking is available everywhere on the Strip and at many downtown casino hotels; this allows you to drive right up to the front of the hotel and stroll inside, and the attendants will fetch your car for you when you're finished, though you may have to wait up to 15 minutes for it to appear if a show has just let out. (Be sure to tip a buck or two.) Otherwise, you can use the cavernous, multilevel self-park garages built at the rear of every casino property, on the Strip or downtown. The downside of self-parking is that the walk into the casino can often be a long one. Every casino has security guards patrolling the parking areas.

Public transportation... Citizens Area Transit (CAT) operates modern, handicapped-accessible buses over a comprehensive system of routes from 5:30am to 1:30am; one-way fares is $1 for adults, 50¢ for children. The one special service is route 301, which runs along the Strip 24 hours a day, originating at the Downtown Transportation Center (corner of Stewart and 4th streets) and continuing past all the major casino hotels to the intersection of Sunset and Las Vegas Boulevard. Route 301's buses run every 10 minutes (every 15 minutes from 12:30am to 5:30am); one-way fare is $1.50 for adults, 50¢ for kids. Some off-Strip hotels also have free shuttle services around town, for guests only.

Safety... Las Vegas has its share of mean streets, but the Strip and downtown's Fremont Street aren't a problem. Uniformed and undercover cops patrol these tourist districts assiduously, and the casino hotels all have their own security guards playing Big Brother, scanning everything from the parking lots to the elevators. Pickpockets do work the heaviest crowds (e.g., pedestrian walkways of major intersections, Fremont Street during the nightly light show, outside the Mirage and Treasure Island during their volcano and pirate-ship shows), so keep your wallet, purse, or backpack where you can see it.

Taxis... Cabs wait like buzzards outside each casino hotel's front entrance 24 hours a day. The meter drops at $2.40, after which you pay 35¢ per 1/5 mile, plus 35¢ per minute of waiting. (It's no wonder most people prefer walking from one Strip hotel to another, even when the temperature hits triple digits.) Here are the names of some local cab companies: **Checker Star Yellow** (tel 702/873–2000); **Desert Cab** (tel 702/376–2687); **Western Cab** (tel 702/736–8000); and **Whittlesea Blue Cab** (tel 702/384–6111).

Tickets... Once upon a time, not very long ago, you could only buy show tickets on the evening of a performance by queuing up in front of the showroom's imperious maître d' and slipping him any number of bills (nothing less than a 10-spot); the denomination dictated where you sat. Even today, when every casino hotel sells tickets straightforwardly through its own box office, at a few showrooms (the Tropicana, the Stardust, the Riviera, Caesars Palace) a well-greased palm might still wedge you into the theater for a sold-out show, or at least get you out from behind that potted palm. On weekend nights, ticket availability is tighter than a showgirl's spandex costume. During the week, though, you should have far fewer problems with last-minute purchases, unless some huge convention is in town. For production shows, the casino hotels' box offices will either sell you a ticket in person or accept a tele-phoned reservation with a credit card number (these seats are held at their "will call" window). Just call the hotel's main number and ask to be transferred to the box office. Ticket policies vary from show to show and casino to casino, so the best strategy is to phone each box office and ask its procedure. You can—and should—purchase tickets to any production well in advance. Some of the most popular and longest-running shows (Siegfried & Roy, for instance) are sold far in advance, but if you line up at the showroom's box office early in the morning on the day of the performance, you may be able to snag a couple of seats through last-minute cancellations. If you want to see a blockbuster show, the soundest advice is to phone the box office as soon as you've planned your trip. In fact, you might as well book those seats before you book the plane and hotel. Concerts at venues such as the Hard Rock, the Aladdin, and the Las Vegas Hilton (as well as a few production shows) also use **Ticketmaster** (tel 702/474–4000) to distribute their seats. Purchasing a seat through Ticketmaster assures you of an assigned seat, while many (but not all) of the casino hotel box offices simply guarantee general admission. If you've got a general admission ticket, line up early for the best seats, and keep a couple of bucks handy to grease the usher. If you're reserving tickets by phone with a credit card, ask whether or not that particular show has assigned seating, and plan accordingly. At other local theater, dance, and music events, tickets are sold through the venue's box office; sell-outs are usually not a problem.

Travelers with disabilities... Parking spaces are set aside in every parking lot; elevators and ramps are built into each nightclub, casino gambling area, restaurant, and lounge; and automatic doors are provided at all entrances. All CAT buses are wheelchair accessible, too (see "Public transportation," above). Wheelchair rentals are available on the Strip through the **Landmark Pharmacy** (tel 702/731–0041; 252 Convention Center Dr.).

Visitor information... The **Las Vegas Convention & Visitors Authority** (tel 702/892–0711, 800/332–5333; 3150 Paradise Rd., Las Vegas 89109) has a very helpful multilingual staff and offers discount coupon books, brochures, and excellent maps.